Praise for David Barsamian's interviews

David Barsamian is the Studs Terkel of our generation.

—Howard Zinn

David Barsamian is one of the great journalists of our era, and a giant of community and public radio.

—Robert McChesney

Praise for Arundhati Roy's essays

The scale of what Roy surveys is staggering. Her pointed indictment of India's hydroelectric industry—which has very little to show for the destruction it has wrought—is devastating.

—*New York Times Book Review*

Arundhati Roy combines brilliant reportage with a passionate, no-holds-barred commentary. I salute both her courage and her skill.

—Salman Rushdie

W.B. Yeats wrote that "the best lack all conviction, while the worst are full of passionate intensity," but Roy is an exception. She overflows with Passionate Conviction.
—*San Francisco Chronicle*

Arundhati Roy's essays evoke a stark image of two Indias being driven "resolutely in opposite directions," a small India on its way to a "glittering destination" while the rest "melts into the darkness and disappears"—a microcosm of much of the world, she observes, though "in India your face is slammed right up against it." Traced with sensitivity and skill, the unfolding picture is interlaced with provocative reflections on the writer's mission and burden, and inspiring accounts of the "spectacular struggles" of popular movements that "refuse to lie down and die." Another impressive work by a fine writer.
—Noam Chomsky

Writers have proved when they turn their back to power and start to feel the pulse and pain of society, they become powerful. This is the power beyond power that Arundhati Roy brings forth in *Power Politics*.
—Vandana Shiva

THE CHECKBOOK AND
THE CRUISE MISSILE

CONVERSATIONS WITH

ARUNDHATI ROY

Interviews by David Barsamian

South End Press
Cambridge, Massachusetts

First edition.
Printed by union workers on acid-free, 20% post-consumer recycled paper.

Library of Congress Cataloging-in-Publication Data
Barsamian, David.
  The checkbook and the cruise missile : conversations with Arundhati Roy /
by David Barsamian and Arundhati Roy.— 1st ed.
     p. cm.
  Includes bibliographical references and index.
  ISBN 0-89608-710-7 (pbk. : alk. paper) — ISBN 0-89608-711-5 (lib. bdg. :
alk. Paper)
  1. Globalization. 2. World politics—1989- 3. International relations. 4.
India—Politics and government—1977- 5. United States—Politics and
government—2001- 6. Roy, Arundhati—Interviews. 7. Indian
authors—Interviews. I. Roy, Arundhati. II. Title.
JZ1318 .B366 2004
327—dc22
                                        2003025639

South End Press, 7 Brookline Street, #1
Cambridge, MA 02139-4146
www.southendpress.org

09 08 07 06 05 04   1 2 3 4 5 6 7

 196

327
B

CONTENTS

ARUNDHATI ROY: WORD WARRIOR

BY NAOMI KLEIN

On March 7, 2003, two weeks before the United States invaded Iraq, Arundhati Roy sent me an essay she had just written. The subject line was "My Last Words: A Submission in Anger." It arrived at the perfect time: despite the unprecedented outpouring of opposition to the attack, the cable stations were giddily counting down to war as if it were New Year's Eve. If there was ever a moment when the world needed a dose of Arundhati Roy's rage and wisdom, it was now.

It took one sentence before I realized that the article was a fake, not written by Roy but by someone out to discredit her. The giveaways were phrases like this: "zombie fascists" to de-

The Checkbook and the Cruise Missile

scribe the citizens of the United States, "the greatest artistic performance in modern history" to describe the September 11 attacks on the World Trade Center.

My heart broke for Arundhati when I read those words. All a writer has is her voice, her words. And here was Roy's precious voice being stolen, violated, made to espouse views she pours her life energy into resisting. But the counterfeit was also strangely instructive: when Roy's enemies set out to destroy her, they do so by trying to rob her of the very thing that makes her powerful—her unfailing humanity, her refusal to give in to easy hatreds, her clear and furious condemnation of all forms of terror.

With her writing and her actions, Roy has placed herself in opposition to anyone who treats people as collateral damage—of a mega-dam, a terrorist attack, or a military invasion. As the attack on Afghanistan began, she wrote: "Nothing can excuse or justify an act of terrorism, whether it is committed by religious fundamentalists, private militias, people's resistance movements—or whether it's dressed up as a war of retribution by a recognized government."[1] And Roy has chosen the very moments when the U.S. government is engaged in its most barbaric acts to reach out to the people of the United States, to make clear distinctions between citizens and states, to try to understand the fear—of outsiders, of each other—that bestows on U.S. politicians so much undeserved power.

Unable to goad her into a politics of hate, Roy's political opponents have resorted to faking it, inventing Arundhati Imposters to do their dirty work. But there's a hitch: Roy's enemies can't write, a serious liability when trying to imitate one of the finest writers of our time, and I have yet to meet a single person who fell for the fake.

I have described Arundhati as a great humanist, but that, of course, is only part of the story. Roy's generosity has its limits—and thank goodness for that. Because if she were only about peace and love, the world would be denied one of its great pleasures: watching Arundhati Roy wage a bloody war of words against U.S. President George W. Bush. He says, "You are either with us, or you are with the terrorists"; she says that we don't have to choose between "a malevolent Mickey Mouse and the Mad Mullahs."[2] He says, "We're a peaceful nation"; she says, "Pigs are horses. Girls are boys. War is peace."[3] He says the invasion of Iraq was right and just because we caught Saddam Hussein; she says that's like "deifying Jack the Ripper for disembowelling the Boston Strangler."[4]

I don't know how Arundhati comes up with these killer one-liners, but I'm grateful. Each one is a gift, capable of transforming fear and confusion into courage and conviction. In Roy's hands, words are weapons—weapons of mass movements. But Roy's essays and speeches are not propaganda, quite the opposite: they are attempts to name our world as it is, exactly, precisely, perfectly. It is for this reason that I sometimes fear that Arundhati will be driven mad by George Bush and the violence he inflicts on the English language. Recently, Roy wrote that she imagined Noam Chomsky watching an American cable news show with an "amused, chipped-tooth smile."[5] I imagine Roy watching that same program with a great roll of tape, picking up the words George Bush has ruthlessly severed from their meanings—peace, evil, war, democracy, truth, good, innocent, justice...—and carefully, urgently, taping them back together again.

The conversations in this book span three years, a period in which Roy invented a new way to be a political activist, not only in India, where she lives, but also in the heart of empire itself, the United States. As Roy tells David Barsamian, it is usually white people who travel south to tell black and brown people who they are. When the travel flows are reversed, the voices from the South are usually personal testimonials about poverty and suffering back home. Roy, however, is occupying a very different cultural space; she is, in her words, "a black woman from India speaking about America to an American audience."[6] Elsewhere, Roy has claimed this right because the United States is not merely a country but the hub of empire.

Foreword by Naomi Klein

"[M]ay I clarify that I speak as a subject of the U.S. empire? I speak as a slave who presumes to criticize her king."[7]

It is Roy's deep understanding of the mechanics of power that is her greatest contribution to movements against neo-liberalism and war. Again and again, Arundhati has used her gifts as a novelist and trained architect to help us visualize the invisible architecture of modern empire. Crucially, she has helped us to understand how powerful interests that seem to be in conflict—the nation state vs. corporate globalization; religious fundamentalism vs. U.S. capitalism—actually serve to strengthen and protect each other, and join forces to lay waste to democracy. In these pages, Roy describes the Indian elite's embrace of corporate globalization and the rise of Hindu nationalism as "a pincer action. With one hand they're selling the country out to multinationals. With the other they're orchestrating this howling cultural nationalism."[8]

According to Roy, all imperial projects—whether political, economic, or religious—share a logic, the logic of bigness. In her essay "The Greater Common Good," she writes of "[b]ig bombs, big dams, big ideologies, big contradictions, big countries, big wars, big heroes, big mistakes."[9] It is this tyranny of scale, Roy tells Barsamian here, that systematically seizes power away from communities and delegates it to centralized governments, and further away still, to global institutions like the World Bank and the World Trade Organization. "The distance between power and powerlessness, between those who take decisions and those who have to suffer those decisions, has increased enormously.... The further and further away geographically decisions are taken, the more scope you have for incredible injustice. That is the primary issue."[10] Our job, Roy tells us, is to narrow the distance, to bring power and decision-making closer to home. For me, this simple mission has become a kind of barometer for my activism: our opponents hoard power, we disperse it.

The press is forever dwelling on Roy's beauty and poise, but she describes herself in less precious terms as a "hooligan."[11] I never believed it until I met her, but it's true. Roy is a natural anti-authoritarian, not only in theory but also in practice: she is incapable of deferring to authority, whether to George W. Bush or to India's Supreme Court (a crime which landed her in jail for "contempt"). It is this total absence of deference that Roy's power-worshipping enemies find so endlessly maddening, and that the rest of us find so limitlessly inspiring.

At the 2003 World Social Forum in Porto Alegre, Brazil, Roy delivered a now legendary speech titled "Confronting Empire." At the end of her talk, Roy played with the Forum's slogan, telling the crowd of tens of thousands that, "Another world is not only possible, she's on her way....[O]n a quiet day, if I listen very carefully, I can hear her breathing."[12] That stadium has never heard silence like that. For weeks after, all of us—from the most hard-core anarchists to the most staid socialist politicians—were firmly under Arundhati's spell, convinced we too could hear that quiet breathing, and utterly determined to turn it into a global roar.

One month later, we did just that: on February 15, we filled the streets of our cities with the largest and most unified rejection of war the world has ever seen. These demonstrations "really stripped down empire," Roy tells Barsamian. "It stripped off the mask."[13] But by the final conversation in this book, readers will notice that Roy is getting impatient. While we are straining to hear our other world, our opponents are building theirs with terrifying determination, employing whatever weapons are required, whether the IMF's checkbook or the Pentagon's cruise missile. There is value to this brazenness, Roy says: it lets us know that the time is past for simply unmasking empire, it's time to take it down, "to dismantle its working parts"[14]—starting with the illegal looting of Iraq. "Enough of being right," she says. "We need to win."[15]

Thank you, Arundhati. As usual, the road ahead is being lit up by your bright and furious words.

—January 2004

KNOWLEDGE AND POWER

David Barsamian: Tell me about Kerala where you grew up. It's a singular place in India for many reasons. It's multi-religious, has a high rate of literacy and has been relatively free from the kinds of sectarian violence that plague other parts of the country.

Arundhati Roy: Kerala is a place where great religions coincide. You have Christianity, Hinduism, Islam, and Marxism [laughs]. They all rub each other down and metamorphize into something new. Politically Kerala is quite volatile. This might mean a clash between the Marxists and the right-wing Hindu nationalist Rashtriya Swayamsevak Sangh [RSS] or between different Communist parties, though it's relatively free of the kind of caste

---

This interview was conducted while driving from Amherst to Boston, Massachusetts, February 16, 2001. An earlier version of this conversation was published in *The Progressive*, April 2001.

1

killing that you have in states like Bihar or Uttar Pradesh.[1] When I first came to North India, it was almost like visiting a different century. Still, Kerala is a complex society because it's progressive and parochial simultaneously. Even among the Syrian Christians—who are the oldest, most orthodox Christians in India—you have caste issues. If you look at the Communist parties, most of their leaders are upper-caste. When they fight elections, candidates are carefully chosen to represent the dominant caste of their respective "vote bank"—an example of how communism will harness the traditional caste system in its quest for power in a "representative" democracy.

Kerala is known for its high literacy rate, but the quality of the education itself is execrable. Kerala University is among the worst universities in India.

I don't think that something like the Narmada valley development project could easily happen in Kerala.[2] That kind of mass injustice—the eviction of hundreds of thousands of people—might be hard to pull off. On the other hand, the first thing E.M.S. Namboodiripad did when he came to power as head of the first democratically elected Communist government in the world was to get Birla, the big industrial group, to set up a huge rayon factory in Calicut.[3]

In the last thirty years that factory has denuded the bamboo forest, poisoned the Chaliyar river, and polluted the air. There is a high incidence of cancer among the local people and the factory workers. The factory is Kerala's biggest private industry, and Kerala, being Kerala, has thirteen trade unions. In the name of employing three thousand people it destroyed the livelihood of hundreds of thousands who lived on these natural resources, fishermen, bamboo workers, sand quarriers. (They don't qualify as "workers" in the Communist dictionary.) The government and courts did nothing about it. Eventually the factory closed down on its own because it had finished off all the raw material there and wanted to move elsewhere.

Because Kerala is so riven with internecine politics, everybody disagrees with everybody else. There are hundreds of factions, and eventually everything remains frozen in a sort of political rigor mortis.

What's the status of women generally in Kerala? Is it different from the rest of India given the high levels of education?

Arundhati Roy and David Barsamian

I know that people say that fertility rates have dropped in Kerala because of literacy.[4] It's probably true. But you have only to watch Malayalam cinema to feel sick to your stomach at the way women are treated and the way women behave. When I was a child, every film I saw had the heroine being raped. Until I was about fifteen, I believed that every woman gets raped. It was just a question of waiting for yours to happen. That was the kind of terror that was inculcated in young girls.

My mother is very well known in Kerala because in 1986 she won a public interest litigation case. She challenged the Syrian Christian inheritance law that said that a woman can inherit one-fourth of her father's property or five thousand rupees, whichever is less. The Supreme Court ruling in her case gave women equal inheritance with retrospective effect from 1956. But actually no women go to court to claim this right. Everyone said, "You can't have it going back to 1956 because the courts will be flooded with complaints." It didn't happen. The churches had will-making classes. They taught fathers how to disinherit their daughters. It's a very strange kind of oppression that happens there. Women from Kerala work all over India and all over the world. Many of the world's nuns and nurses are from Kerala. They send all the money they earn back home to support their families. And yet the nurses, who earn comparatively huge salaries, will get married, pay a dowry, and end up having the most bizarrely subservient relationships with their husbands.

Growing up in a little village in Kerala was a nightmare for me. All I wanted to do was to escape, to get out, to never have to marry somebody there. Not that people were queuing to marry me [laughs]. I was worst thing a girl could be: thin, black, and clever. No looks, no dowry, no good.

Your mother, Mary, also broke the unofficial love laws.

She married a Bengali Hindu and then, what's worse, divorced him, which meant that everyone was confirmed in their opinion that it was a terrible thing to marry for love—outside the community.

What was it like growing up without a father at home?

In Kerala everyone has what is called a *tharavaad*, your ancestral home. If you don't have a father, you don't have a *tharavaad*. You're a person without an address. "No address," that's what they call you. I grew up in Ayemenem, the village in which *The God of Small Things* is set.[5] Given the way things have turned out, it's easy for me to say that

I thank God that I had none of the conditioning that a normal middle-class Indian girl would have. I had no father, no presence of this man "looking after" us and beating or humiliating our mother occasionally in exchange. I had no caste, no religion, no supervision.

It was made very clear to me early on by everyone around me that I would not be given the protection that other children around me had. Anything could have happened to me. I could have gone under. But because I didn't, I have a vantage point from which to watch what's going on now. I'm not rural, not urban, not completely "traditional" nor wholeheartedly "modern." I grew up in a village. I saw rural India at work. And yet I had the advantage of having an education. It's like being at the top of the bottom of the heap—without the blinkered single-mindedness of the completely oppressed nor the flabby self-indulgence of the well-to-do. There must be very few girls in India whose mothers say, "Whatever you do, don't get married. And don't sleep with a man until you're financially independent." It was sound advice— not that I listened [laughs]. When I see brides all dressed up for the sacrifice, it gives me a rash. I find them ghoulish, almost. I find what that whole thing means in India so frightening—to see this decorated, bejeweled creature willingly, happily entering a life of permanent subjugation.

You're close to your mother today?

I left home when I was sixteen, for all sorts of reasons, and didn't see her for many years. Like many mothers and daughters, we had a complicated relationship—nothing to do with our politics, though. My mother is like someone who strayed off the set of a Fellini film. But to have been brought up by a woman who never made it her mission in life to find another partner to entwine herself around is a wonderful thing.

My mother runs a school in the town of Kottayam. It's phenomenally successful. People try to book their children into it before they are even born. Yet folks in town don't know quite what to make of her. Or me. The problem is that we are both women who are unconventional. The least we could have done was to be unhappy. But we aren't. That's what bothers people: the fact that you can make these choices and be happy—like a pair of witches.

My mother's school is very unconventional. She started it with five or six students when I was about four or five. She managed to persuade the Rotary Club of

Kottayam to rent us their premises in the daytime. In the morning we would put up tables and be taught how to read and write. In the evening the men would meet and smoke and leave all their cigarette butts and teacups and whisky glasses all over. Middle-class Indian men leave their rubbish everywhere for others to clean up. The next morning we would clean it all up and then it would be the school. I used to call it a sliding, folding school. People know that the education children get from my mother's school is invaluable. And yet it makes them uncomfortable because she's not amenable to all the rules and regulations of their society.

Now it's complicated even further by what has happened to me since *The God of Small Things* was published. I was the first student from her school. In a way she's vindicated—it's like a B-grade film script. Suffering, belief, and hard work, then beautiful retribution. You can't imagine that something like this could happen: the way we were treated by that town, the way things were when I was a child, compared to now. Even the book, people don't know how to deal with it. They want to embrace me and to say that this is "our woman," and yet they don't want to address what the book is about, which is their society and its intrinsic, callous brutality. They have to find ways of filtering out the parts they don't want to address. They have to say it's a book about children, something like that.

You were the target of a criminal case in Kerala because someone said The God of Small Things *was obscene.*

I was charged with corrupting public morality [laughs]. As though public morality was pure until I came along. I was at the high court in Cochin a year or two ago. I had appealed to have the case quashed, saying that for a number of reasons it wasn't legally valid. The lawyers of both sides were ready to argue but the judge came on and said, "I don't want to hear this case. Every time it comes up before me I get chest pains" [laughs]. He postponed the hearings, and the case still sits there in court.

Since you wrote your novel, you've produced some remarkable political essays. What was that transition like, from writing in the world of fiction and imagination to writing about concrete things, like dams, people being displaced in the Narmada valley, globalization, and Enron?

It's only to other people that it appears to be a transition. When I was in fourth year in architecture school, I already knew that I would never practice architecture because it involves being a part of a chain of such ugly exploitation. I couldn't do it. I was very interested in urbanization and town planning, in how a city comes to be what it is and what it does to those who live in it.

I've been doing this kind of work since I was twenty-one. It's only to the outside world, those who came to know me after *The God of Small Things*, that it seems like a transition. I wrote political essays before I wrote the novel. I wrote three essays called "The Great Indian Rape Trick" (in two parts) and "The Naughty Lady of Shady Lane" about the way the film *Bandit Queen* exploited Phoolan Devi and whether or not somebody should have the right to restage the rape of a living woman without her consent.[6]

I don't see a great difference between *The God of Small Things* and my nonfiction. In fact, I keep saying, fiction is the truest thing there ever was. Today's world of specialization is bizarre. Specialists and experts end up severing the links between things, isolating them, actually creating barriers that prevent ordinary people from understanding what's happening to them. I try to do the opposite: to create links, to join the dots, to tell politics like a story, to communicate it, to make it real. To make the connection between a man with his child telling you about life in the village he lived in before it was submerged by a reservoir, and the WTO, the IMF, and the World Bank. *The God of Small Things* is a book which connects the very smallest things to the very biggest. Whether it's the dent that a baby spider makes on the surface of water in a pond or the quality of the moonlight on a river or how history and politics intrude into your life, your house, your bedroom, your bed, into the most intimate relationships between people—parents and children, siblings and so on.

If you lose these connections, everything becomes noise, meaningless, a career plan to be on track for tenure. It's a bit like the difference between allopathy and homeopathy or any other form of indigenous medicine. You don't just treat the symptoms. You don't just say, "Oh, you've got a patch on your skin, so let me give you some steroids." You ask, "Why do you have it? How has it come there? What does it mean? What are you thinking about today? Are you happy? Why has your body produced this?" You can't just be a skin expert. You must understand the human body and the human mind.

You've talked about the colonization of knowledge and its control and a Brahmin-like caste that builds walls around it. What do you think the relationship should be between knowledge and power and politics?

All over the world today people are fighting for a right to information. The organizations that control the world today—the WTO, the IMF, the World Bank—operate in complete secrecy. Contracts that goverments sign with multinationals, which affect people's lives so intimately, are secret documents. For example, I think that the contract between Enron, the giant Houston-based energy corporation, and the government of Maharashtra should be a public document. It is the biggest contract ever signed by the Indian government. It guarantees this one corporation profits that add up to more than sixty percent of India's rural development budget.[7] Why is it a secret document? Who is the government to sign away its public buildings as collateral? The government holds everything, whether it's the natural resources or the Rashtrapati Bhavan, the President's residence in New Delhi, in trust for the people that it represents. It cannot sign these things away. That contract must be a public document. That's one aspect of the relationship between knowledge and power.

The Checkbook and the Cruise Missile

But there is a more insidious aspect. It isn't a coincidence that four hundred million Indian people are illiterate. When I say "illiterate," I don't want to imply that the kind of education that is being imparted is literacy. Education sometimes makes people float even further away from things they ought know about. It seems to acutally obscure their vision. The kind of ignorance that people with Ph.D.s display is unbelievable. When the Supreme Court judgment about the Narmada valley came out in October 2000, I wrote an analysis of what it meant.[8] Then I went to the valley. People were marching. They were so angry, they desecrated a copy of the judgment and buried it. There was a public meeting at which many Adivasis and farmers spoke. A friend of mine said, "Isn't it amazing that there isn't a single point that you have brought up that they're not already talking about with the same sophistication?" I said, "No, we're the ones who have to make the leap of faith. For them, it's their lives."

The Supreme Court judgment transforms their lives. It's not an intellectual exercise. It's not research. If you see how far away people who are educated and have become consultants or experts or whatever have floated from what's happening, I think you'll see the entire "development" debate is a scam. The biggest problem is that what they say in their project reports and what actually happens are two completely different things. They've perfected the art of getting it right on paper, but that has nothing to do with what is happening on the ground.

The distance between power and powerlessness, between those who take decisions and those who have to suffer those decisions, has increased enormously. It's a perilous journey for the poor—it's a pitfall filled to overflowing with lies, brutality, and injustice. Sitting in Washington or Geneva in the offices of the World Bank or the WTO, bureaucrats have the power to decide the fate of millions. It's not only their decisions that we are contesting. It's the fact that they have the power to make those decisions. No one elected them. No one said they could control our lives. Even if they made great decisions, it's politically unacceptable.

Those men in pin-striped suits addressing the peasants of India and other poor countries all over again—assuring them that they're being robbed for their own good, like long ago they were colonized for their own good—what's the difference? What's changed? The further and further away geographically decisions are taken, the more scope you have for incredible injustice. That is the primary issue.

The power of the World Bank is not only its money, but its ability to accumulate and manipulate knowledge. It probably employs more Ph.D.s than any university in the world. It funds studies that suit its purpose. Then it disseminates them and produces a particular kind of worldview that is supposedly based on neutral facts. But it's not. It's not at all. How do you deal with that? What is the difference between that and the Vishwa Hindu Parishad [VHP] or the Bharatiya Janata Party [BJP] openly rewriting history texts and saying that we will now give you the Hindu version of history?[9] The World Bank version of development is the same thing.

The Narmada valley project envisions the construction of something like three thousand large and medium dams along the course of the Narmada River and its tributaries. It covers three states, Maharashtra, Gujarat, and Madhya Pradesh. There's been a resistance movement to what was originally a World Bank scheme. The World Bank has now withdrawn from the project and the government of India has taken it over. Tell me about the Narmada Bachao Andolan [NBA], the Save the Narmada Movement.

The remarkable thing about the NBA is that it is a cross-section of India. It is the Adivasis, the upper-caste big farmers, the Dalits, and the urban middle class. It's a forging of links between the urban and the rural, between farmers, fishermen, writers, painters, and lawyers. That's what gives it such phenomenal strength.

When dam proponents in India say, "You know, these middle-class people, they are against development and they're exploiting illiterate farmers and Adivasis," it makes me furious. After all, the whole Narmada Valley Development Project was dreamed up by the middle-class mind. Middle-class urban engineers designed it. You can't expect the critique to be just rural or Adivasi. People try to delegitimize the involvement of the middle class, saying, "How can you speak on behalf of these people?" No one is speaking on behalf of anyone. The criticism of middle-class dam opponents is an attempt to isolate the Adivasis, the farmers, and then crush them. After all, government policy documents aren't in Hindi or Bhilali, and the Indian Supreme Court doesn't work in Hindi or Bhilali.

The NBA is a fantastic example of a resistance movement in which people link hands across caste and class. It is India's biggest, finest, most magnificent resistance movement since the independence struggle succeeded in the 1940s. There are other resistance movements in India. It's a miracle that they exist. But I fear for their future.

When you travel from India to the West, you see that the Western notion of "development" has to do with a lack of imagination. A taming of the wilderness, of the human soul. An inabilty to understand that there is another way to live. In India, the anarchy and the wilderness still exist (though they're under the hammer). But still, how are you going to persuade a Naga sadhu—whose life mission has been to stand naked on one leg for twenty years or to tow a car with his penis—that he can't live without Coca-Cola? It's an uphill task.

Estha, one of the characters in your novel, walks "along the banks of the river that smelled of shit and pesticides bought with World Bank loans."[10]

When I first met activists from the NBA, they told me, "We knew that you would be against big dams and the World Bank when we read *The God of Small Things.*" I've never had that kind of a reading before [laughs].

In India, the whole pesticide issue is just unbelievable. The Green Revolution, bringing canal irrigation, bore

17

wells, and chemical pesticides and fertilizer, has now led to serious problems. After a point, the productivity of the land begins to diminish. That has started happening in places like Andhra Pradesh, where farmers have been forced to abandon traditional farming and grow cash crops. Now that move has backfired because of the import of food grains under new WTO rules. Hundreds of farmers in Punjab and Andhra Pradesh are committing suicide because of their growing debt. They have to invest more and more in pesticides and fertilizers. Pests have grown resistant to the chemicals. The farmers have to make large capital investments to force a little bit of productivity out of these dead lands. They end up killing themselves by drinking pesticide.

Arrogant interventions in ecosystems that you don't understand can be ruinous. In the northeast of India, some states started exporting frog legs to France. It became a big earner of foreign exchange. As the frogs began to disappear, the pests they used to eat began to destroy crops. The states started having to buy pesticides (with World Bank loans), which eventually cost more than the money they made by exporting frog legs.

The Checkbook and the Cruise Missile

I think it was in Tanzania that farmers began to shoot hippos because they were raiding and destroying the crops. When the hippos disappeared, so did the fish in the river. Later they discovered that these fish used to lay their eggs in the shit of the hippos. When human beings don't respect something that they don't understand, they end up with consequences that you cannot possibly foretell.

The Western notion of thinking that you must understand everything can also be destructive. Why can't we just be satisfied with not understanding something? It's all right. It's wonderful to not understand something. To respect and revere the earth's secrets.

There was a particular mountain in the Himalayas that hadn't ever been climbed. Some climbers wanted to climb it. I had a friend who led a campaign to allow that one peak to remain unclimbed. There's a kind of humility in that. I don't mean to take an extreme position and say that science is bad. But there ought to be a balance between curiosity, grace, humility, and letting things be. Must everything be poked at and prodded and intervened in and understood?

Arundhati Roy and David Barsamian

Proponents of the Narmada valley project say that it will bring water to the thirsty and crops to the parched land of three states. What's wrong with that?

I've written about this extensively in my essay "The Greater Common Good."[11] They say the Sardar Sarovar Dam is going to take water to Kutch and Saurashtra, the regions of Gujarat which were the hardest hit by the earthquake in January 2001. They have a terrible drought in these areas. But if you look at the government's own plans, you'll see there is no possibility that the water will get to these regions, even if everything that they say were to work. For example, they arbitrarily assume an irrigation efficiency of sixty percent. No irrigation project has ever been more than thirty-five percent efficient in India. Kutch and Saurashtra are right at the tail end of this big canal system, but all the politically powerful areas are right up at the head of the canal. They will take away all the water. Already big sugar factories have been licensed before the dam has been built. According to the project, sugar was not going to be allowed to be planted. Huge five-star hotels and golf courses have been built.

Even if all this hadn't happened, according to the Gujarat government's own plan, the Sardar Sarovar Dam will irrigate 1.2 percent of the cultivable area of Kutch and nine percent of Saurashtra. That's forgetting about the irrigation efficiency and the sugar factories, about the fact that rivers close to Kutch and Saurashtra are being dammed and the water is being taken to central Gujarat.

In fact, when the Supreme Court judgment came and the Gujarat BJP government had a huge ceremony to inaugurate the beginning of the construction of the dam, Kutch and Saurashtra boycotted it. They said, "You are just using us to mop up eighty-five percent of Gujarat's irrigation budget—and in the process not leaving any money for local water harvesting or for more local solutions to this problem."

That's one thing. The second is that they don't even ask, "Why is there a drought in Kutch and Saurashtra?" The reason is that the government has systematically cut down all the mangrove forests. They have mined groundwater indiscriminately and so there's an ingress of seawater from the coast. They have big industrial complexes that poison whatever groundwater remains. The Gujarat government will do nothing, nothing at all to control this kind of thing.

If they want to take water from the Narmada to Kutch just to make a political statement, of course they can, but it will be as a circus—an economically unviable political circus—like taking red wine or champagne to Kutch. Narmada is so far away from Kutch and Saurashtra that it's a joke to take all that water all the way up through Gujarat. For the price of the Sardar Sarover Dam, you could finance local water harvesting schemes in every single village in the state of Gujarat.[12]

What prompted the World Bank to pull out of the project?

The peoples' resistance movement in 1993 and 1994. The World Bank was forced to set up an independent review. They sent out a committee under a man named Bradford Morse. The Morse Report, which is now a kind of landmark, said in no uncertain terms that the Bank should pull out. Of course the Bank tried to cover up the report. It sent another committee, the Pamela Cox Committee, which tried to say everything's fine. But Morse had agreed that he would do this study only provided it was an independent report. Finally the World Bank was forced to pull out.[13] This is unprecedented in the murky history of the World Bank.

The Checkbook and the Cruise Missile

The government of India seems to be determined to complete the Narmada project. What's driving it?

First of all, you must understand that in India the myth of big dams is sold to us from the time we're three years old. In every school textbook, we learn that Pandit Nehru said "dams are the temples of modern India."[14] Criticizing dams is equated with being anti-national.

The thing about dams and the struggle against them is that people have to understand that they're just monuments to corruption and they are undemocratic. They centralize natural resources, snatch them away from people, and then redistribute them to a favored few.

The first dam built on the Narmada was in Madhya Pradesh, the Bargi Dam, which was completed in 1990. They said it would displace seventy thousand people and submerge one hundred and one villages. One day they just filled the reservoir. One hundred and fourteen thousand people, almost twice the government's projection, were displaced and one hundred and sixty-two villages were submerged. They were just driven from their homes when the waters rose. They had to run up the hill with their cattle and children. Ten years later, that dam irrigates five percent of the land that they said it would. It irrigates less land than it submerged.

In Gujarat, the Sardar Sarovar Dam has been used by every political party as a campaign issue for years. The amount of disinformation about this dam is extraordinary. For contractors and politicians, just the building of the dam makes them a lot of money.

Forty percent of the big dams that are being built in the world today are in India. Tens of millions of Indians have already been displaced by many of the dam projects.[15] *What happens to these people? What kind of resettlement or compensation is provided by the government?*

Nobody knows. When I was writing *The Greater Common Good,* what shocked me more than the figures that do exist and are thrown around and fought over by pro-dam and anti-dam activists are the figures that don't exist. The Indian government does not have any estimate of how many people have been displaced by big dams. I think that's not just a failure of the state, but a failure of the intellectual community. The reason that these figures don't exist is that most of the displaced are the non-people, the Adivasis and the Dalits.

The Checkbook and the Cruise Missile

I did a sanity check based on a study of fifty-four dams done by the Indian Institute of Public Administration. According to that study, the number of reservoir-displaced, which is only one kind of displacement, came to an average of something like forty-four thousand people per dam. I said, "Let's assume that these fifty-four dams are the bigger of the big dams. Let's *quarter* this average, and say each dam displaced ten thousand people. We know that India has built thirty-three hundred big dams built in the last fifty years. So just a sanity check says that it's thirty-three million people displaced." At the time I wrote this, people mocked this figure. Now, the India Country Study done by the World Commission on Dams puts that figure at as much as fifty-six million.[16]

Today, India doesn't have a national resettlement policy. The government of Madhya Pradesh, where eighty percent of Sardar Sarovar-displaced people are from, gave a written affidavit in court saying it did not have enough land to resettle people. The Supreme Court still ordered the construction of the dam to go ahead.

What happens to the people who are driven out from their villages by these development projects and by the general garrotting of India's rural economy? They all migrate to the cities. And there, again, they are non-citizens, living in slums. They are subject to being evicted at a moment's notice, any time a new office complex or a five-star hotel chain covets the land they live on.

You compare the uprooting of these people to a kind of garbage disposal.

That's exactly what it is. The Indian government has managed to turn the concept of nonviolence on its head. Nonviolent repression. Unlike, say, China or Turkey or Indonesia, the government of India doesn't mow down its people. It doesn't kill people who refuse to move. It just continues to pursue the brutal path of this particular model of "development" and to ignore the consequences. Because of the caste system, because of the fact that there is no social link between the people who make the decisions and the people who suffer the decisions, it just goes ahead and does what it wants. It's quite an efficient way of doing things. India has a very good reputation in the world as a democracy, as a government that cares. But, that's just not true.

But you say about your own politics that you're "not an anti-development junkie nor a proselytizer for the eternal upholding of custom and tradition." [17]

The Checkbook and the Cruise Missile

How can I be? As a woman who grew up in a village in India, I've spent my whole life fighting tradition. There's no way that I want to be a traditional Indian woman. So I'm not talking about being against development. I'm talking about the politics of development. I'm talking about more development, not less. More democracy, not less. More modernization, not less. How do you break down this completely centralized, undemocratic process of decision-making? How do you make sure that it's decentralized and that people have power over their lives and their natural resources? I don't even believe in the modern business-like notion of "efficiency." It dovetails with totalitarianism, fascism. People say, "If it's decentralized it will be inefficient." I think that's fine. Let it be inefficient.

Today the Indian government is trying to present privatization as the alternative to the state, to public enterprise. But privatization is only a further evolution of the centralized state, where the state says that they have the right to give the entire power production in Maharashtra to Enron. They don't have the right. The infrastructure of the public sector in India has been built up over the last fifty years with public money. They don't have the right to sell it to Enron. They cannot do that.

You say private enterprise is going to be more efficient? Look at what Enron is doing. Is that efficient? The same thing is happening in the telecom sector.

Three-quarters of our country lives on the edge of the market economy.[18] You can't tell them that only those who can afford water can have it.

Talk about the material you covered in your essay, "The End of Imagination":[19] *the nuclear testing in India, followed by Pakistan. You say in India the official reasons given for the testing are threats from China and Pakistan and exposing Western hypocrisy.*

When India carried out the nuclear tests May 1998, within weeks the Pakistani infiltration of Kargil in Kashmir began. The Indian government didn't do anything about it because they knew how embarrassing it would be to actually admit that the nuclear tests triggered a war. So they allowed it to happen. Hundreds of soldiers got killed.[20] The Indian government and the mainstream media used the Kargil War to whip up more patriotism. It's so frightening, the nationalism in the air in India. I'm terrified by it. It can be used to do anything.

The Checkbook and the Cruise Missile

Some of the cheering young Hindu men who were thrilled with the destruction of the Babri mosque in Ayodhya in the northern state of Uttar Pradesh were also celebrating the nuclear tests.

And the same ones were protesting about Coke. The same Bal Thackeray of Shiv Sena who met Rebecca Mark of Enron and signed the thirty-billion-dollar deal wants to ban birthday parties and Valentine's Day because they are an attack on Indian culture.[21] Indian intellectuals today feel radical when they condemn communalism, but not many people are talking about the link between privatization, globalization, and communalism. Globalization suits the Indian elite. Communalism doesn't. It doesn't create a good "investment climate." I think they have to be addressed together, not separately. They are both two sides of the same coin. Growing religious fundamentalism is directly linked to globalization and to privatization. The Indian government is talking about selling its entire power sector to foreign multinationals, but when the consequences of that become hard to manage, the government immediately starts saying, "Should we build the Ram temple in Ayodhya?" Everyone goes baying off in that direction. Meanwhile, contracts are signed.

It's like a game. That's something we have to understand. It's like a pincer action. With one hand they're selling the country out to multinationals. With the other they're orchestrating this howling cultural nationalism. On the one hand you're saying that the world is a global village. On the other hand governments spend millions and millions patrolling their borders with nuclear weapons.

You use a metaphor of two convoys of trucks, one very large one with many people going off in the darkness and another, much smaller, going into the digital promised land.[22]

Every night outside my house in New Delhi I pass this road gang of emaciated laborers digging a trench to lay fiber optic cables to speed up our digital revolution. They work by the light of a few candles. That is what is happening in India today. The convoy that melts into the darkness and disappears doesn't have a voice. It doesn't exist on TV. It doesn't have a place in the national newspapers. And so it doesn't exist. The people that are in the little convoy on their way to this glittering destination at the top of the world don't care to see or even acknowledge the larger convoy heading into the darkness.

The Checkbook and the Cruise Missile

In Delhi, the city I live in, the cars are getting bigger and sleeker, the hotels are getting posher, the gates higher. The guards outside houses are no longer the old *chowkidars*, watchmen, they are young fellows with uniforms. And yet everywhere the poor are packed like lice into every crevice in the city. People don't see that any more. It's as if you shine a light very brightly in one place, the darkness deepens around it. They don't want to know what's happening. The people who benefit from this situation can't imagine that the world is not a better place.

It's part of that regular diet of contradictions that Indians live with. You made a decision, or the decision was made for you, to identify with, or to be part of, that large convoy.

I can't be a part of the large convoy because it's not a choice that you can make. It's a choice that's made by your circumstances. The fact that I'm an educated person means that I can't be on that convoy. I'm too privileged. Besides, I don't want to be on it. I don't want to be a victim. I don't want to disappear into the darkness. I don't want anyone to disappear into the darkness.

You talk passionately about taking sides, about not being a neutral observer reporting on events in a distant way.

Once you've seen certain things, you can't un-see them, and saying nothing is as political an act as speaking out. There is no innocence. That I'm sure about. There's no innocence and there isn't any sense in which any of us is perfect or not invested in the system. If I put money in a bank it's going to fund the bombs and the dams. When I pay tax, I'm investing in projects I disagree with. I'm not a completely blameless person campaigning for the good of mankind. But from that un-pristine position, is it better to say nothing or to say something? One is not powerful enough nor powerless enough not to be invested in the process. Most of us are completely enmeshed in the way the world works. All our hands are dirty.

I read somewhere that you once lived in a squatter's colony within the walls of Delhi's Ferozeshah Kotla in a small hut with a tin roof, scrounging beer bottles to sell.

That's true. But it's not tragic. It was fun [laughs]. As I said, I left home when I was sixteen. I had to put myself through college. So I used to live there because the mess manager of the canteen in the school of architecture hostel had this little hut. Ferozeshah Kotla was right next to my college. I used to live there with my boyfriend and a whole lot of other people who could not afford to live in the hostel.

What was your experience working in the film industry in India?

I worked on a few films that were a part of the lunatic fringe, films that no one really wanted to see. It wasn't at all part of the film industry. It was very marginal.

Some of these stories that you're telling about resistance and the NBA would seem to be grist for a film or a television series. Is anything like that going on in India?

No. There are a lot of documentary films. Few of them transcend the boundaries between activism and art. I think there are tremendous stories for making film, like the Bhopal tragedy that Union Carbide was responsible for. But I'm a loner. I can't bear the idea of working with a film crew, negotiating with the producer, actors and all the rest of it. I've done it—it's not my thing.

You could write a screenplay.

But then they'll fuck it up [laughs]. One of the things about writing *The God of Small Things* was that I negotiated with nobody. It was just me and my book. A fantastic way to spend four and a half years of my life. No negotiations.

Arundhati Roy and David Barsamian

In January 2000, in a village on the banks of the Narmada, there was a protest against the Maheshwar Dam. You were among many who were arrested there.

The Maheshwar Dam, which is the dam upstream from the Sardar Sarovar, is India's first private hydro electric project. Its chief promoter is a textile company called S. Kumars. The resistance managed to kick out a whole host of private companies, starting with U.S. companies like Pacgen and Ogden, then German firms like Siemens and HypoVereinsBank. Last year, the villagers decided that they were going to take over the dam site.

I was in the valley in a village called Sulgaon. All night, people were arriving from the surrounding villages, by tractor, by jeep, on foot. By three in the morning there were about five thousand of us. We started walking in the dark to the dam site. The police knew that the dam site would be captured, but they didn't know from where the people would come.

It was unforgetable. Five thousand people, mostly villagers, but also people from the cities, lawyers, architects, journalists, walking through these byways and crossing streams in absolute silence. There was not a person that lit a bidi or coughed or cleared their throats.

The Checkbook and the Cruise Missile

Occasionally a whole group of women would sit down and pee and then keep walking. Finally, at dawn, we arrived and took over the dam site. For hours, the police surrounded us. Then there was a *lathi*, baton, charge. They arrested thousands of people, including me. They dumped me in a private car that belonged to S. Kumars. It was so humiliating. The jails were full. Because I was there at that time, there was a lot of press and less violence than usual. But people have captured the Maheshwar Dam site so many times before, and it doesn't even make it to the news.

What is the status of the Narmada valley project now that the Supreme Court decision of October 2000 has granted permission for the completion of the Sardar Sarovar Dam in the state of Gujarat?

The status is totally uncertain. Gujarat is in shambles from the earthquake last month. What is happening there is ugly. The Gujarat government, and its goon squad the VHP, is commandeering all the relief money. There are reports of how Muslims, Christians, and Dalits are being left out of the reconstruction efforts. In Bhuj, one of the worst-hit towns, they have seventeen different categories of tents for the seventeen different castes. It's infuriating to think of how much money these guys must have received from international donors and what they will end up using it for.

Everyone is keeping very quiet about what effect the earthquake will have on the dam. Sardar Sarovar is on a fault line. This is a point that's been brought up again and again. Everybody's ignored it.[23]

The Vishwa Hindu Parishad or VHP is the religious arm of the ruling party, the BJP.

It's a sort of extreme right wing. There's the RSS, and even more right-wing than the RSS is the VHP. Even further to the right is the Bajrang Dal. They are the ones burning churches, destroying mosques, and killing priests.[24]

You make the connection between the rise of extreme Hindu-based nationalism and globalization. Are there any local factors at work here?

There are plenty of local factors, but for me this connection explains how disempowerment works. When you have dispossession and disempowerment on this scale as a result of corporate globalization, the anger that it creates can be channeled in bizarre and dangerous ways. India's nuclear tests were conducted to shore up people's flagging self-esteem. India is still flinching from the cultural insult of British colonialism, still looking for its identity. It's about all that.

Are you thinking about writing any more fiction?

I need to write fiction like you need to eat or exercise, but right now it's so difficult. At the moment, I don't know how to manage my life. Just one writer who says quite simply to the people in the Narmada valley, "I'm on your side" leads to so much love and so much affection and so many people asking you to join them. Just the fact that you're known as somebody who's willing to speak out opens you to a universe of conflict and pain and incredible suffering. It's impossible to avert your eyes. Sometimes, of course, it becomes ludicrous. A woman rang me up and said, "Oh, darling, I thought that piece on the Narmada was fantastic. Now could you do one for me on child abuse?" I said, "Sure. For or against?"

People just assume you're a gun for hire, you can write about anything. I don't know how I'll ever be able to make the space to say, "I'm writing a book now, and I'm not going to be able to do" x or y. I would love to.

You are a celebrity within India and also outside. How do you handle this?

As a rule I never do things because I'm a celebrity. Also I never avoid doing things because I'm a celebrity. I try to ignore that whole noisy production. Of course I have the whole business of people asking me to inaugurate this or that. I never do that. I stand by what I write. That's what I am—a writer. If I began to believe the publicity about myself, whether for or against, it would give me a very absurd idea of myself. I know that there's a very fine balance between accepting your own power with grace and misusing it.

When I say my own power, I don't mean as a celebrity. Everybody, from the smallest person to the biggest, has some kind of power, and even the most powerless person has a responsibility. I don't feel responsible for everybody. Everybody also is responsible for themselves. I don't ever want to portray myself as a representative of the voiceless or anything like that. I'm scared of that.

You were attacked from the left for The God of Small Things *and from the right for "The End of Imagination."*[25] *There's a little cottage industry of anger springing up around you.*

The pillars of society can't decide whether I'm extreme left, extreme right, extreme Green, or an extremely bad writer.

The Checkbook and the Cruise Missile

Gandhi called India's independence "a wooden loaf." Many of the issues plaguing the Subcontinent are rooted in its partition. What's your perspective on relations between India and Pakistan. India is a multi-cultural, multi-layered country and has one of the largest Muslim populations in the world.

Partition has left a huge and bloody legacy between India and Pakistan. I think both countries are doing their best to keep it alive. The reasons for this range from actual communal hatred and religious suspicion, to governments and bureaucrats making money off arms deals. They use this manufactured conflict and hypernationalism to gain political mileage in their own countries.

I sense some optimism on your part on what you call the "inherent anarchy" of India to resist the tide of globalization.

I don't know whether to be optimistic or not. When I'm outside the cities, I do feel optimistic. In India, unlike perhaps many other countries which are being broken by these new forms of colonialism, there is such grandeur. Ultimately, people prefer to eat roti and idlis and dosas rather than McDonald's burgers. Whether it's Indian food or textiles, there's so much beauty. I don't know whether they can kill it. I want to think they can't. I don't think that there is anything as beautiful as a sari. Can you kill it? Can you corporatize a sari?

Just before I came here, I went to a market in Delhi. There was a whole plate of different kinds of rajma dal, lentils. Today, that's all it takes to bring tears to your eyes, to look at all the kinds of rajma that there are, all the kinds of rice, and think that they don't want this to exist.

They want to privatize it and control the seeds.

They want to do the same to cultures and people and languages and songs. Globalization means standardization. The very rich and the very poor must want the same things, but only the rich can have them.

TERROR
AND THE MADDENED KING

It's been nineteen months since our last interview. Can you up-date me on the criminal case filed against you in a district magistrate's court in Kerala for your book, The God of Small Things. *The charge was "corrupting public morality."* [1] *What has been the out-come of that particular case?*

Well, it hasn't had an outcome. It's still pending in court, but every six months or so the lawyer says, "There's going to be a hearing; can you please come?"

This is one of the ways in which the state controls people. Having to pay a lawyer, or having a criminal case in court, never knowing what's going to happen. It's not about whether you get sentenced eventually or not. It's

This text is based on two interviews conducted in Albuquerque, New Mexico and Las Vegas, Nevada, on September 19 and 29, 2002.

the harassment. It's about having it on your head, about not knowing what will happen.

More recently you've been charged and found guilty of contempt of court by India's Supreme Court, apparently in response to your criticism of its decision to allow construction to proceed on the Narmada valley dam project. You could have been sentenced to six months in jail but they gave you only a symbolic one-day sentence and a small fine.

It's McCarthyism—a warning to people that criticizing the Supreme Court could jeopardize your career. You'd have to hire lawyers, make court appearances—and eventually you may or may not be sentenced. Who can afford to risk it?

Tell me about Aradhana Seth's film, called "DAM/AGE." [2]

Usually when people ask me to make films with them, I refuse. The request to do "DAM/AGE" came just after the final Supreme Court hearing, when it became pretty obvious to me that I was going to be sentenced, one way or another. I didn't know for how long. I was pretty rattled, and thought that if I was going to be in jail for any length of time, at least my point of view ought to be out in the world.

The Checkbook and the Cruise Missile

In India, the press is terrified of the court. So there wasn't any real discussion of the issues. It was discussed in a "Cheeky Bitch Taken to Court" sort of cheap, sensationalist way, but not seriously. After all, what is contempt of court? What does this law mean to ordinary citizens? None of these things had been discussed at all. So I agreed to do the film simply because I was nervous, and wanted people to know what this debate was about.

In a very moving segment of the film, you discuss a man named Bhaiji Bhai. Can you talk about him?

Bhaiji Bhai is a farmer in Gujarat, from a little village called Undava. When I first met him, I remember thinking, "I know this man from somewhere." I had never met him before. Then I remembered that a friend of mine who had made a film on the Narmada years before had done an interview with Bhaiji Bhai. He had lost something like seventeen of his nineteen acres to the irrigation canal in Gujarat. And because he had lost it to the canal, as opposed to submergence in the reservoir area, he didn't count as a project-affected person, and wasn't compensated. So he was pauperized, and had spent I don't know how many years telling strangers his story. I was just another stranger that he told his story to, hoping that some day someone would intervene and right this great wrong that had been done to him.

Women seem to be central to the struggle in the Narmada valley. Why do you think women are so actively engaged there?

Women are actually actively engaged in many struggles in India. And especially in the Narmada valley. In the Maheshwar Dam submergence villages, the women of the valley are particularly effective. Women are more adversely affected by uprootment than men. Among the Adivasi people, it is not the case that men own the land and women don't. But when Adivasis are displaced from their ancestral lands, the meager cash compensation is given by the government to the men. The women are completely disempowered. Many are reduced to offering themselves as daily laborers on construction sites, and they are exploited terribly. Women often realize that if they're displaced, they are more vulnerable, and therefore they understand the issues in a more visceral and deeper sense than the men do.

You write in your latest essay, "Come September," that the theme of much of what you talk about is the relationship between power and powerlessness. And you write about "the physics of power." [3] *I'm interested that you use that term, physics. It kind of connects with the mathematical term you used in another of your essays, "The Algebra of Infinite Justice." What do you have in mind there?*

Unfettered power results in excesses such as the ones we're talking about now. And eventually, that has to lead to structural damage. I am interested in the physics of history. Historically, we know that every empire overreaches itself and eventually implodes. Then another one rises to take its place.

But do you see those excesses as inherent in the structure of power? Are we talking about something inevitable here?

Inevitable would be too fatalistic a term. But I think unfettered power does have its own behavioral patterns, its own DNA. When you listen to George Bush speak, it's as though he has no perspective because he's driven by the crazed impulse of a maddened king. He can't hear the murmuring in the servants' quarters. He can't hear the words of the world's subjects. He's driving himself into a situation and he cannot turn back.

Yet, just as inevitable as the journey that the powerful undertake is the journey undertaken by those who are engaged in the business of resisting power. Just as power has a physics, those of us who are opposed to power also have a physics. Sometimes I think the world is divided into those who have a comfortable relationship with power and those who have a naturally adversarial relationship with power.

You've just spent a couple of weeks in the United States. You spoke in New York and Santa Fe, then took a driving trip through parts of New Mexico. What do you think about the incredible standard of living that Americans enjoy, and the price that is exacted from the developing world to maintain that standard of living?

It's not that I haven't been to America or to a Western country before. But I haven't lived here, and I can't seem to get used to it. I haven't got used to doors that open on their own when you stand in front of them, or looking at these supermarkets stuffed with goods. But when I'm here, I have to say that I don't necessarily feel, "Oh, look how much they have and how little we have." Because I think Americans themselves pay such a terrible price.

In what way?

In terms of emotional emptiness. Watching Michael Moore's film, "Bowling for Columbine," you suddenly get the feeling that here is a country with an economy that thrives on insecurity, on fear, on threats, on protecting

46

what you have—your washing machines, your dishwashers, your vacuum cleaners—from the invasion of killer tomatoes or evil women in saris or whatever other kind of alien.[4] It's a culture under siege. Every person who gets ahead gets ahead by stepping on his brother, or sister, or mother, or friend. It's such a sad, lonely, terrible price to pay for creature comforts. I think people here could be much happier if they could let their shoulders drop and say, "I don't really need this. I don't really have to get ahead. I don't really have to win the baseball match. I don't really have to come first in class. I don't really have to be the highest earner in my little town." There are so many happinesses that come from just loving and companionship and even losing.

You write in your essay "Come September," that the Bush administration is "cynically manipulating people's grief" after September 11 "to fuel yet another war—this time against Iraq."[5] *You're speaking out about Iraq and also Palestine. Why?*

Why not?

But you know that those are stories that are very difficult for most Americans to hear. There's not a lot of sympathy in the United States for the Palestinians, or for the Iraqis, for that matter.

47

But the thing is, if you're a writer, you're not polling votes. I'm not here to tell stories that people want to hear. I'm not entering some popularity contest. I just say what I have to say, and the consequences are sometimes wonderful and sometimes not. But I'm not here to say what people want to hear.

Let's talk a little bit about the mass media in the United States. You write that "thanks to America's 'free press,' sadly, most Americans know very little" about the U.S. government's foreign policy.[6]

Yes, it's a strangely insular place, America. When you live outside it, and you come here, it's almost shocking how insular it is. And how puzzled people are—and how curious, now I realize, about what other people think, because it's just been blocked out. Before I came here, I remember thinking that when I write about dams or nuclear bombs in India, I'm quite aware that the elite in India don't want to know about dams. They don't want to know about how many people have been displaced, what cruelties have been perpetrated for their own air conditioners and electricity. Because then the ultimate privilege of the elite is not just their deluxe lifestyles, but deluxe lifestyles with a clear conscience. And I felt that that was the case here too, that maybe people here don't want to know about Iraq, or Latin America, or Palestine, or East Timor, or Vietnam, or anything, so that they can live this happy little suburban life. But then I thought about it. Supposing you're a plumber in Milwaukee or an electrician in Denver. You just go to work, come home, you work really hard, and then you read your paper or watch CNN or Fox News and you go to bed. You don't know what the American government is up to. And ordinary people are maybe too tired to make the effort, to go out and really find out. So they live in this little bubble of lots of advertisements and no information.

Third World Resurgence, an excellent magazine out of Penang, Malaysia, had a recent article on the Bhopal disaster of 1984. More than half a million people were seriously injured and some three thousand people died on December 3, 1984, when a cloud of lethal gas was released into the air from Union Carbide's Bhopal facility in central India. More than twenty thousand deaths have since been linked to the gas.

The article features a leader among Bhopal survivors named Rasheeda Bee—you can tell from the name she's Muslim—who lost five members of her immediate family to cancer after the disaster, and she herself continues to suffer from diminished vision, headache, and panic. At the Earth Summit in Johannesburg a few weeks ago, Rasheeda tried to personally hand over a broom to the president of Dow Chemical, which has now taken over Union Carbide, and here's what she said: "The Indian Government has received clear instructions from its masters in Washington, D.C. The [Indian] government has made it clear to us [that is, the victims] that if it comes to choosing between holding Dow [Chemical] / [Union] Carbide liable (or punishing Warren Anderson [who was the CEO of Union Carbide]) and deserting the Bhopal survivors, it will opt for the latter without batting an eyelid."7

Even the absurd compensation that the Indian courts agreed upon for the victims of Bhopal has not been disbursed over the last eighteen years. And now the governments are trying to use that money to pay into constituencies where there were no victims of the Bhopal disaster.8 The victims were primarily Muslim, but now they're trying to pay that money to Hindu-dominant constituencies, to look after their vote banks.

You were speaking to some students in New Mexico recently and you advised them to travel outside the United States, to put their ears against the wall and listen to the whispering. What did you have in mind in giving them that kind of advice?

The Checkbook and the Cruise Missile

That when you live in the United States, with the roar of the free market, the roar of this huge military power, the roar of being at the heart of empire, it's hard to hear the whispering of the rest of the world. And I think many U.S. citizens want to. I don't think that all of them necessarily are co-conspirators in this concept of empire. And those who are not, need to listen to other stories in the world—other voices, other people.

Yes, you do say that it's very difficult to be a citizen of an empire. You also write about September 11. You think that the terrorists should be "brought to book." But then you ask the questions, "Is war the best way to track them down? Will burning the haystack find you the needle?" [9]

Under the shelter of the U.S. government's rhetoric about the war against terror, politicians the world over have decided that this technique is their best way of settling old scores. So whether it's the Russian government hunting down the Chechens, or Ariel Sharon in Palestine, or the Indian government carrying out its fascist agenda against Muslims, particularly in Kashmir, everybody's borrowing the rhetoric. They are all fitting their mouths around George Bush's bloody words. After the terrorist attack on the Indian Parliament on December 13, 2001, the Indian government blamed Pakistan (with no evidence to back its claim) and moved all its soldiers to the border. War is now considered a legitimate reaction to terrorist strikes. Now through the hottest summers, through the bleakest winters, we have a million armed men on hair-trigger alert facing each other on the border between India and Pakistan. They've been on red alert for months together. India and Pakistan are threatening each other with nuclear annihilation. So, in effect, terrorists now have the power to ignite war. They almost have their finger on the nuclear button. They almost have the status of heads of state. And that has enhanced the effectiveness and romance of terrorism.

The U.S. government's response to September 11 has actually privileged terrorism. It has given it a huge impetus, and made it look like terrorism is the only effective way to be heard. Over the years, every kind of nonviolent resistance movement has been crushed, ignored, kicked aside. But if you're a terrorist, you have a great chance of being negotiated with, of being on TV, of getting all the attention you couldn't have dreamt of earlier.

When Madeleine Albright was the U.S. ambassador to the United Nations in 1994, she said of the United States, "We will

The Checkbook and the Cruise Missile

behave multilaterally when we can and unilaterally when we must." I was wondering, in light of the announcement last week [on September 17] of the Bush doctrine about preemptive war, if that may not be used as legitimacy for, let's say, India to settle scores with Pakistan.[10] *Let's say the Bharatya Janata Party [BJP] government in New Delhi says, "Well, we have evidence that Pakistan may attack us, and we will launch a preemptive strike."*

If they can borrow the rhetoric, they can borrow the logic. If George Bush can stamp his foot and insist on being allowed to play out his insane fantasies, then why shouldn't Prime Minister A.B. Vajpayee or Pakistan's General Musharraf? In any case, India does behave like the United States of the Indian Subcontinent.

You know the old expression, "Beauty is in the eye of the beholder." Maybe "terrorist" is the same thing. I'm thinking, for example, Yitzhak Shamir and Menachem Begin were regarded by the British as terrorists when they were controlling Palestine. And today they're national heroes of Israel. Nelson Mandela was considered for years to be a terrorist, too.

In 1987, when the United Nations wanted to pass a resolution on international terrorism, the only two countries to oppose that resolution were Israel and the United States, because at the time they didn't want to recognize

53

the African National Congress and the Palestinian struggle for freedom and self-determination.[11]

Since September 11, particularly in the United States, the pundits who appear with boring regularity on all the talk shows invoke the words of Winston Churchill. He's greatly admired for his courage, and he's kind of a model of rectitude to be emulated. In "Come September," you have a very unusual quote from Winston Churchill, that often does not get heard anywhere. Can you paraphrase it?

He was talking about the Palestinian struggle, and he basically said, "I do not believe that the dog in the manger has the right to the manger, simply because he has lain there for so long. I do not believe that the Red Indian has been wronged in America, or the Black man has been wronged in Australia, simply because they have been displaced by a higher, stronger race." [12]

And he said this in 1937, I believe.

Yes.

You conclude your essay, "War Is Peace," by wondering: [H]ave we forfeited our right to dream? Will we ever be able to re-imagine beauty?" [13]

That was written in a moment of despair. But we as human beings must never stop that quest. Never. Regardless of Bush or Churchill or Mussolini or Hitler, or whoever else. We can't ever abandon our personal quest for joy and beauty and gentleness. Of course we're allowed moments of despair. We would be inhuman if we weren't, but let it never be said that we gave up.

Vandana Shiva, who's a prominent activist and environmentalist in India, told me a story once about going to a village, and trying to explain to the people there what globalization was doing to people in India. They didn't get it right away, but then somebody jumped up and said, "The East India Company has come back." So there is that memory of being colonized and being recolonized now under this rubric of corporate globalization. It's like the sahibs are back, but this time not with their pith helmets and swagger sticks, but with their laptops and flow charts.

We ought not to speak only about the economics of globalization, but about the *psychology* of globalization. It's like the psychology of a battered woman being faced with her husband again and being asked to trust him again. That's what is happening. We are being asked by the countries that invented nuclear weapons and chemical weapons and apartheid and modern slavery and racism—countries that have perfected the gentle art of genocide, that colonized other people for centuries—to trust them when they say that they believe in a level playing field and the equitable distribution of resources and in a better world. It seems comical that we should even consider that they really mean what they say.

In "DAM/AGE" there's an incredibly moving scene where the Supreme Court in New Delhi is surrounded by people who have come from the Narmada valley and elsewhere and are chanting your name and giving you support. There was just so much love and affection, and tears came to your eyes. As I recount it, I'm getting the chills myself. It was very beautiful.

I was very scared that day. Now that it's over it's okay to say what I'm saying. But while it was happening, while I was surrounded by police, and while I was in prison—even though I was in prison for a day—it was enough to know how helpless one can be. They can do anything to you when you are in prison.

I knew that people from the Narmada valley had come. They hadn't come for me personally. They had come because they knew that I was somebody who had said, with no caveats, "I'm on your side." I wasn't hedging my bets like most sophisticated intellectuals, and saying, "On the one hand, this, but on the other hand, that." I was saying, "I'm on your side." So they came to say, "We are on your side when you need us."

The Checkbook and the Cruise Missile

I was very touched by this, because it's not always the way people's movements work. People don't always come out spontaneously onto the streets. And one of the things about resistance movements is that it takes a great deal of mobilization to keep a movement together and to keep them going and to do things for one another. There are so many different kinds of people putting their shoulders to the wheel. It's not as though all of them have read *The God of Small Things*. And it's not as if I know how to grow soya beans. But somewhere there is a joining of minds and a vision of the world.

.

David Barsamian and Arundhati Roy in New Delhi, India, November 2002. Photos © by Sanjay Kak.

PRIVATIZATION
AND POLARIZATION

You just finished writing an introduction to Noam Chomsky's
For Reasons of State, *which is being reissued after being out of
print for several years.*[1] *What did you learn as you read his essays?*

The one fact that shocked me was that Chomsky had
searched mainstream U.S. media for twenty-two years for
a single reference to American aggression in South Vietnam, and had found none. At the same time, the "free
world" is in no doubt about the fact that the Russians invaded Afghanistan, using exactly the same model, the
same formula—setting up a client regime and then invit-
ing themselves in. I'm still taken aback at the extent of

This interview was conducted in New Delhi on November 20
and 21, 2002.

indoctrination and propaganda in the United States. It is as if people there are being reared in a sort of altered reality, like broiler chickens or pigs in a pen. In India, the anarchy and brutality of daily life means there are more free spaces, simply because it's impossible to regulate. People are beyond the reach of the bar code. This freedom is being quickly snatched away. Reading Chomsky gave me an idea of how unfree the free world is, really. How uninformed. How indoctrinated.

Why did you call your introduction "The Loneliness of Noam Chomsky"?

There was a poignant moment in an old interview when he talked about being a fifteen- or sixteen-year-old boy in 1945 when the atomic bomb was dropped on Hiroshima. He said that there wasn't a single person with whom he could share his outrage. And that struck me as a most extreme form of loneliness. It was a loneliness which evidently nurtured a mind that was not willing to align itself with any ideology. It's interesting for me, because I grew up in Kerala, where there was a Communist government at the time of the war in Vietnam. I grew up on the cusp between American propaganda and Soviet propaganda, which somehow canceled each other out.

The Checkbook and the Cruise Missile

Really the line is between the citizen and the state, regardless of what ideology that state subscribes to. Even
now in India, or anywhere else, the minute you allow the
state to take away your freedoms, it will. So whatever freedoms a society has exist because those freedoms have
been insisted upon by its people, not because the state is
inherently good or bad. And in India and all over the
world, freedoms are being snatched away at a frightening
pace. I think it's not just important but urgent for us to
become extremely troublesome citizens, to refuse to allow the state to take away what it is grabbing with both
hands just now.

*In your essay "Come September" you write that in country after
country, freedoms are being curtailed in the name of protecting freedom. In the United States, there's the USA PATRIOT Act, and
you have something similar in India, called PoTA, the Prevention of
Terrorism Act.² Do you see any similarities?*

Terrorism has become the excuse for states to do just
what they please in the name of protecting citizens against
terrorism. Hundreds of people are being held in prisons
under the antiterrorism law in India. Many of them are
poor people, Dalits and Adivasis, who are protesting
against "development projects" that deprive them of

their lands and livelihoods. Poverty and protest are being conflated with terrorism. There was a fake "encounter" in New Delhi's Ansal Plaza just a couple weeks ago, on November 3. The police claimed that they had foiled a terrorist attack, and that the people they killed were Pakistani terrorists. But from eyewitness reports, it's pretty clear that that police story was concocted.[3]

Similarly, on the thirteenth of December—soon after the September 11 attack in New York—there was an attack on the Indian Parliament. Five men were killed on the spot. Nobody knows who they really were. The government, as usual, claims they were Pakistanis. They've held four additional suspects in prison for almost a year now: a Kashmiri Muslim professor from Delhi University, two other Kashmiri Muslim men, and a woman who's Sikh, but married to Shaukat Ali, one of the accused. During the trial, it seemed as if almost every piece of evidence had been manufactured by the police. As for the professor, Syed Abdul Rehman Geelani, there's no evidence whatsoever to support his arrest. All three men have been sentenced to death. It's outrageous.[4]

In March 2000, just before Bill Clinton came here, there was a massacre of Sikhs in Chittisinghpura in the

valley of Kashmir. The police claimed they killed terrorists who were responsible for the massacre. It now turns
out that the people they killed were not terrorists, but just
ordinary, innocent villagers. The chief minister of Kashmir actually admitted that the DNA samples that were
sent to a lab for testing were fake. But nothing happens.
You've killed these people, you've admitted to fudging
the DNA samples, but nothing happens. Holes are blown
into every bit of evidence, but nothing happens.[5]

There's been the Tehelka scandal. The secretary of
the BJP, Bangaru Laxman, and the secretary of the
Samata Party, Jaya Jaitley, were caught on film accepting
bribes for fake arms deals. Nothing happens.[6] So there's
this kind of marsh into which everything sinks. A citizen's
rights are such a fragile thing now.

*A few years ago there was a major massacre of Sikhs right here
in the capital of India. Thousands of Sikhs were killed after the assassination of Indira Gandhi. And in Bombay after the Babri
Masjid was destroyed in Ayodhya, several thousand Muslims were
massacred.*[7]

Yes, and nothing happened. And in Gujarat now,
Narendra Modi is spearheading an election campaign,
and the Congress Party and the BJP are both openly talk-

ing about playing the Hindu card, or using the caste card vs. the Hindu card. So we have to ask ourselves, What is the systemic flaw in this kind of democracy that makes politicians function by creating these vote banks divided along caste lines, or communal lines, or regional lines. As I wrote in my essay "Democracy: Who Is She When She Is at Home?" democracy is India's greatest strength, but the way in which electoral democracy is practiced is turning it into our greatest weakness.[8]

We both attended a solidarity meeting on behalf of Professor Geelani, who teaches Arabic at Delhi University, and you are on the committee in his support. I'm sure you're besieged with requests to be on such-and-such a committee, to write a letter, to do this and that. How do you make those kinds of choices?

I use my instinct, because that's the only thing I can do. I understand clearly and deeply that no individual matters all that much. It doesn't matter all that much eventually what I do and what I don't do. It matters to me. I can help as much as I can help. But ultimately it isn't the way a battle must be fought—by the support of one individual or another. I don't believe in that kind of celebrity politics.

The Checkbook and the Cruise Missile

I just continue to do what I've always done, which is
to write, to think about these things. I'm searching for an
understanding. Not for my readers, for myself. It's a process of exploration. It has to further my understanding of
the way things work. So in a way it's a selfish journey, too.
It's a way of pushing myself further and deeper into looking at the society in which I live. If I were to be doing it
not as an exploratory thing, but just as a politician might,
with some fixed agenda, and then trying to convince people of my point of view, I think I'd become jaded.
Curiosity takes me where it takes me. It leads me deep
into the heart of the world.

After the publishing of The God of Small Things, *you
could have had your pick of any publisher in New York. I'm sure
they were clamoring for you. Yet you chose a small, independent press
based in Cambridge, Massachusetts, South End Press, to publish*
Power Politics *and, coming up,* War Talk. *Was that that kind
of spontaneous, instinctive choice you made?*

It wasn't some big policy decision on my part. I didn't
even think at the time, actually, that this is a political step.
But I use my political instincts a lot. It's important for me
to stay that way. People really imagine that most people
are in search of fame or fortune or success. But I don't

65

think that's true. I think there are lots of people who are more imaginative than that. When people describe me as famous and rich and successful, it makes me feel queasy. Each of those words falls on my soul like an insult. They seem tinny and boring and shiny and uninteresting to me. It makes me feel unsuccessful because I never set out to be those things. And they make me uneasy. To be famous, rich, and successful in this world is not an admirable thing. I'm suspicious of it all.

Failure attracts my curiosity as a writer. Loss, grief, brokenness, failure, the ability to find happiness in the saddest things—these are the things that interest me. I don't want to play out the role of someone who's just stepped out of "The Bold and the Beautiful." At the same time, it is interesting to be able to meditate on wealth and fame and success, because I have them, and I can play with them, disrespect them, if you know what I mean. I don't suppose that if you haven't been there, you fully understand how empty it all is, in so many ways. And yet, there are wonderful things about being a writer who is widely read.

I can go to Korea, to Japan, to South Africa, to Latin America, and I know that I'll meet kindred souls. And they won't be hard for me to find. I won't have to spend ten years looking for them because my writing has preceded me. I'm a paid-up member of SIN—the Sweethearts International Network. It's a bond between people that arises from literature and politics. I can't think of a more wonderful thing. Writing gives you this gift. It plugs you directly into the world.

There used to be a saying in American journalism—it's not being followed today because of the corporatization of the media—that the function of journalists was to comfort the afflicted and afflict the comfortable. In a way, what you're saying seems to mirror that. That you feel that you want to make those people in power uneasy and uncomfortable.

I don't think that people in power become uneasy and uncomfortable. But you can annoy and provoke them. People who are powerful are not people who have subtle feelings like uneasiness. They got there because of a certain capacity for ruthlessness. I don't even consider their feelings when I write. I don't write for them.

That reminds me of something connected with Chomsky. I've attended many of his lectures. He's often introduced as someone who speaks truth to power. I asked him about that once. He said he doesn't do that. He's not interested in that.

Power knows the truth.

He wants to provide information to people who are powerless, not to those who are oppressing them.

Isn't there a flaw in the logic of that phrase—speak truth to power? It assumes that power doesn't know the truth. But power knows the truth just as well, if not better, than the powerless know the truth. Enron knows what it's doing. We don't have to tell it what it's doing. We have to tell other people what Enron is doing. Similarly, the people who are building the dams know what they're doing. The contractors know how much they're stealing. The bureaucrats know how much they're getting as bribes.

Power knows the truth. There isn't any doubt about that. It is really about telling the story. Good fiction is the truest thing that ever there was. Facts are not necessarily the only truths. Facts can be fiddled with by economists and bankers. There are other kinds of truth. It's about telling the story. As a writer, that's the best thing I can do. It's not just about digging up facts.

When I wrote *The God of Small Things,* it isn't just that I had a story, and then told it. The way you tell a story, the form that narrative takes, is a kind of truth, too. When I wrote "The Greater Common Good," it isn't that no one knew these facts before. There were volumes and volumes of books on dams—pro-dam, anti-dam, balanced views, and so on. But really in the end, it's about how you tell that story to somebody who doesn't know it. To me, as a writer, that is something that I take great pleasure in. Telling the story in a way that ordinary people can understand, snatching our futures back from the experts and the academics and the economists and the people who really want to kidnap or capture things and carry them away to their lairs and protect them from the unauthorized gaze or the curiosity or understanding of passers-by. That's how they build their professional stakes, by saying, "I am an expert on something that you can't possibly understand. My expertise is vital to your life, so let me make the decisions."

Who tells the stories is absolutely critical. Who is telling the stories in India today?

This is a very important question. When *The God of Small Things* came out, my mother said to me, "Why did you have to call the village Ayemenem? Why did you have to say the river was the Meenachil?" I said, "Because I want people to know that we have stories." It's not that

India has no stories. Of course we have stories—beautiful and brilliant ones. But those stories, because of the languages in which they're written, are not privileged. So nobody knows them.

When *The God of Small Things* won the Booker Prize, there was a lot of hostility towards me from regional-language writers, people who write in Hindi, Malayalam, Tamil, and Marathi. It was a perfectly understandable hostility. The Indian writers who are well known and financially rewarded are those who write in English—the elite.

All of my political writing is traslated into Indian languages, Gujarati, Malayalam, Tamil, Bengali, Hindi, and so on. Now I have a relationship with the regional press in Kerala, the Hindi press in the North, in Bengal. Now the English-language media is far more hostile to me than the regional media.

It goes on forever, the question of who tells the story. Even within regional-language writing, the Brahmins and the upper caste have traditionally told the stories. The Dalits have not told their stories. There's an endless pecking order.

The Checkbook and the Cruise Missile

Look at, say, the case of Vietnam now. To the world today, thanks to Hollywood and thanks to the U.S. mass media, the war in Indochina was an American war. Indochina was the lush backdrop against which America tested its technology, examined its guilt, worried about its conscience, dealt or did not deal with its guilt. And the "gooks" were just the other guys who died. They were just stage props. It doesn't matter what the story was. It mattered who was telling it. And America was telling it.

In India, I occupy an interesting space. As a writer who lives in India, writes in English, and has grown up in a village in Kerala, I have spent the first half of my life battling traditions, Indian traditions, that wanted me to be a particular kind of Indian woman, which I have refused to be. And now I'm up against the monstrosity of the other side. The monstrosity of the modern world. People like me confront this contradiction. It's a very interesting place to be in, really. Where even politically, you're caught between the fascist regional forces, the BJP and VHP, for instance, versus the monstrous market forces, the Enrons and that Bechtels.

Speaking of Enron, the Houston-based energy giant multinational which was deeply involved in a dam project in Maharashtra, it has collapsed, laying off thousands of workers, most of whom have lost their pensions and retirement benefits. There's been a corporate crime wave in the United States, a huge amount of corruption. You might recall that it wasn't too long ago that the United States was lecturing a lot of the world about having transparency and clear and open procedures. It's rather ironic.

People often don't understand the engine that drives corruption. Particularly in India, they assume government equals corruption, private companies equal efficiency. But government officials are not genetically programmed to be corrupt. Corruption is linked to power. If it is the corporations that are powerful, then they will be corrupt. I think there have been enough studies that show that corruption has actually increased in the era of privatization. Enron, for instance openly boasted about how it paid some twenty million dollars to "educate" Indian politicians.[9] It depends on how you define corruption. Is it just the bribe-taker? Or is the bribe-giver corrupt as well? Today we see a formidable nexus between the powerful elites in the world. Imperialism by e-mail. This time around, the white man doesn't have to go to poor countries and risk diarrhea and malaria or dying in the tropics. He just has his local government in place, which takes charge of "creating a good investment climate." And those who are protesting against privatization and development projects—making investments unsafe—are called terrorists.

You're a critic of corporate globalization. But what kind of arrangements would you like to see, in terms of governance, of relations between different countries?

I am a critic of corporate globalization because it has increased the distance between the people who take decisions and the people who have to suffer those decisions. Earlier, for a person in a village in Kerala, his or her life was being decided maybe in Trivandrum or, eventually, in Delhi. Now it could be in the Hague or in Washington, by people who know little or nothing of the consequences their decisions could have. And that distance between the decision-taker and the person who has to endure or suffer that decision is a very perilous road, full of the most unanticipated pitfalls.

It's not that everything is designed to be malevolent, of course. Most of it is, but the distance between what happens on paper, in policy documents, and what happens on the ground is increasing enormously. That distance has to be eliminated. Decentralization and the

73

devolving of power to local groups is very important. The current process is fundamentally undemocratic.

You have written that "a writer's bad dream" is "the ritualistic slaughter of language." [10] *Can you talk about some examples of how language is constructed.*

The language of dissent has been co-opted. WTO documents and World Bank resettlement policies are now written in very noble-sounding, socially just, politically democratic-sounding language. They have co-opted that language. They use language to mask their intent. But what they say they'll do and what they actually do are completely different. The resettlement policy for the Sardar Sarovar Dam sounds reasonably enlightened. But it isn't meant to be implemented. There isn't the land. It says communities should be resettled as communities. But just nineteen villages from Gujarat have been scattered in one hundred and seventy-five different locations. [11]

The policy's only function is to ease the middle class's conscience. They all say "Oh, how humane the world is now compared to what it used to be." They can't be bothered that there's no connection between what's happening on the ground and what the policy says. So the

74

issue is not how nice the World Bank president is or how wonderfully drafted their documents are. The issue is, who are they to make these decisions?

There's a sequence in "DAM/AGE" in which World Bank President James Wolfensohn is visiting New Delhi, and he comes out to meet some demonstrators from the NBA. He utters a stream of platitudes about how he cares for the poor, how his focus is on alleviating their suffering and their poverty. In the film you say that you couldn't bear to hang around and wait for him to come out of his meeting, to hear that.

I was there when they blockaded the road. It was evening by the time Wolfensohn was forced to come out. He arrived in his pinstripe suit like a cartoon white man coming to address the peasants of India. I couldn't bear to hear or see this played out again. At the end of the twentieth century, to see the White Man back again, addressing the peasants of India and saying how concerned he was about them.

Only a few weeks later, I was in London, at the release of the World Commission on Dams report, and Wolfensohn was there.[12] He talked about how he had met with the people of the valley. Missing from his account were the police and those steel separators, and the fact that he had been dragged out of the office and forced to meet them. He made it sound like a genuine grassroots meeting.

There are some exciting things happening culturally in India. In addition to "DAM/AGE," the documentary by Aradhana Seth, there's another one by Sanjay Kak called "Words on Water," about resistance in the Narmada valley.[13] *Are you encouraged that those kinds of films are being made and seen?*

There are many independent filmmakers who are doing interesting work. But, more important, in India is that there is a vital critique of what is happening. For instance, in Madhya Pradesh there is a huge and growing resistance to the privatization of power. Privatization of the essential infrastructure, water, power, is strangling the agricultural community. Mass protests are building up. The move to corporatize agriculture, the whole business of genetically modified foods, pesticides, cash crops like cotton and soya bean, are crushing the Indian agricultural sector. The myth of the Green Revolution is coming apart. In Punjab, the lands irrigated by the Bhakra Dam are becoming salinized and water-logged. The soil is yielding less and less and the farmers have to use more and more fertilizers. Punjabi farmers, once the most prosperous in India, are committing suicide because they're in debt.

The WTO has now forced India to import rice, wheat, sugar, milk, all these products which India has in abundance. The government's warehouses are overflowing with excess food grains, while people starve. They're all being dumped. In Kerala, coffee, tea, and rubber plantations are closing down, laying off their labor or not paying them.

In India now there is a move toward Hindutva, and more and more communal politics. This hasn't happened overnight. People point to December 6, 1992, when the mosque in Ayodhya, the Babri Masjid, was destroyed by Hindu fundamentalists. But it must have its roots deeper than just ten years ago.

It has its roots in the independence movement. The RSS was set up in the 1920s. Today it is the cultural guild to which L.K. Advani and Vajpayee and all of these people owe allegiance. So the RSS has been working toward this for eighty years now. There is a link between religious fascism and corporate globalization. When you impose corporate globalization onto an almost feudal society, it reinforces inequalities. The people who are becoming more and more prosperous, are the ones who have had social advantages over many, many years. It's the kind of situation in which fascism breeds.

On the one hand, you have the government privatizing everything, selling off the public sector in chunks—telecommunications, water, power—to multinationals. On the other hand, they orchestrate this baying nationalism, nuclearism, communalism. I've talked about this in my essays "Power Politics" and "Come September."

Every day The Times of India *has a quote on the front page, and today's is from George Eliot: "An election is coming. Universal peace is declared, and the foxes have a sincere interest in prolonging the lives of the poultry."* [14] *What do you think about elections as a mechanism for democracy? I ask that because people have had enormous influence and impact outside the electoral system, for example, Gandhi or Martin Luther King, Jr. They never ran for elective office.*

I think it is dangerous to confuse the idea of democracy with elections. Just because you have elections doesn't mean you're a democratic country. They're a very vitally important part of a democracy. But there are other things that ought to function as checks and balances. If elections are the only thing that matter, then people are going to resort to anything to win that election.

The Checkbook and the Cruise Missile

You can only campaign in a particular constitutional framework. If the courts, the press, the Parliament are not functioning as checks and balances, then this is not a democracy. And today in India, they are not functioning as checks and balances. If they were, Narendra Modi would be in jail today. He would not be allowed to campaign for office. Several candidates would be in jail today. Not to mention several senior people in the Congress Party who ought to have been in jail from 1984 onward for their roles in the massacre of Sikhs in Delhi after the assassination of Indira Gandhi.

The good thing about elections is that, however unaccountable politicians are, at least every five years they have to stand for election. But the bureaucracy and the judiciary are completely unaccountable. Nobody understands the terrifying role that the judiciary is playing in India today. The Supreme Court is taking the most unbelievable positions.Its decisions affect the lives of millions of people. Yet to criticize them is a criminal offense.

Recently, the Chief Justice of India, B.N. Kirpal, made an outrageous order on the day before he retired.[15] Out of a case that had nothing to do with linking rivers,

Kirpal ordered that all the rivers in India should be linked up in ten years' time. It was an arbitrary, uninformed order based on a whim—nothing more. He asked state governments to file affidavits. They never did. The government of India filed an affidavit stating that the project would take forty-one years and cost billions of dollars. This kind of decision is almost, if not more, dangerous than communal politics. Yet, because of the contempt of court law, nobody will question the court. Not the press. Everybody's scared of going to jail.

By sending me to jail, think of what they did: I had a one-year criminal trial, for which you have to have a criminal lawyer which costs an unimaginable amount of money. How is any journalist going to afford a one-year criminal trial and then face the prospect of going to jail, of losing his or her job? What editor, which journalist is going to take that risk? So they've silenced the press. And now the courts have started to rule on vital issues like globalization, privatization, river-linking, the rewriting of history textbooks, whether a temple should be built in Ayodhya—every major decision is taken by the court. No one is allowed to criticize it. And this is called a democracy.

The Checkbook and the Cruise Missile

So you're saying that dissent is being criminalized in India.

I'm saying that a democracy has to function with a system of checks and balances. You cannot have an undemocratic institution functioning in a democracy, because then it works as a sort of manhole into which unaccountable power flows. All the decisions are then taken by that institution because that is the one institution that cannot be questioned. So there is a nexus between the judiciary and the executive. All the difficult decisions are being taken by the judiciary, and it looks as if the judiciary is admonishing the executive and saying, "You're very corrupt. We are forced to become an activist judiciary and to take these decisions."

If you speak to the middle class, they believe that the Supreme Court is the only institution that functions properly. There's a sort of hierarchical thinking that the buck must stop somewhere. They *like* the fact that the Supreme Court is so supremely unaccountable.

The contempt of court law is so draconian that if tomorrow I had documentary evidence to prove that a judge was corrupt, and had taken money from somebody to make a particular decision, I couldn't produce that evidence in court because it would constitute contempt of

81

court. It would be seen to be "lowering the dignity of the court," and in such a case, truth is not a defense.

Are there organizations—NGOs—in the country that are working on this issue? The issue of the autocracy of the court?

It's a very important political issue that we need to fight. But few have understood it yet.

This business of NGOs is a very interesting one in India. I'm no great fan of NGOs. Many of them are funded by various Western agencies. They end up functioning like the whistle on a pressure cooker. They divert and sublimate political rage, and make sure that it does not build to a head. Eventually it disempowers people.

In the first interview we did, in early 2001, you described India as two separate convoys, going in different directions. One into the digital future of the promised land of glitzy electronic things, and the rest of the country, the poor, the anonymous, going in the other direction. Since then, do you see those convoys coming closer together, or are they getting more and more distant from each other?

The way that the machine of neoliberal capitalism works, that distance has to increase. If what you have to plow back into the system is always your profit, obviously that distance is going to increase. Just mathematically, it's going to increase. Whoever has more makes more, and makes more and makes more.

Tell me about the current situation in the Narmada valley. It seems that despite the heroic efforts and sacrifices that the NBA and its members and supporters have made, it looks like the dams are going through. Is that assessment correct?

Construction on the Maheshwar Dam has been stopped for now, but the Sardar Sarovar Dam is inching up. That part of the anti-dam movement has really come up against a wall. The question has to be asked: If nonviolent dissent is not viable, then what is?

If reasoned nonviolent dissent is not honored, then by default, you honor violence. You honor terrorism. Because you cannot just put this plastic bag over the head of the world and say, "Don't breathe." Across India insurgents and militants have taken over great swathes of territory where they just won't allow the government in. It's not just Kashmir. It's happening all over: Andhra Pradesh, parts of Bihar, Madhya Pradesh, and almost the whole of the northeast, which doesn't consider itself a part of India.

Arundhati Roy and David Barsamian

Do you see the possibility of the NBA extending itself beyond its current lifespan into a more national movement of resistance? Could it be a model that people could emulate?

People in cities think that the movement has lost. In one sense, they're right, because the Sardar Sarovar Dam is going up. But if you go to the valley, you'll see the great victories of that movement, which are cultural, which are empowering. People know that they have rights. In the Narmada valley, the police cannot treat Adivasis, and in particular Adivasi women, the way they do elsewhere. These are great and important victories. The section of the NBA that was fighting against the Maheshwar Dam are the younger activists in the valley. They have now expanded their operations way beyond the valley and are fighting the privatization of power in the whole state of Madhya Pradesh. They are spearheading the anti-privatization movement.

Do you see any opening for resolving the conflict between India and Pakistan over Kashmir? The Indian Prime Minister has said "Kashmir is ours. They," presumably the Pakistanis or the Kashmiris, "will never get it. That decision has been made." [16] *Tens of thousands of Kashmiris have died. It's a militarized state. There's*

The Checkbook and the Cruise Missile

martial law. There's a suspension of the constitution. You know better than I do about the human rights abuses that go on there.

Kashmir is the rabbit that the governments of both India and Pakistan pull out of their hats whenever they're in trouble. They don't want to resolve the conflict. For them, Kashmir is not a problem; it's a solution. Let's never make the mistake of thinking that India and Pakistan are searching for a solution and haven't managed to find one. They're not searching for a solution, because if they were, you would not hear intractable statements like this—absurd statements like this—being made.

After the nuclear tests that India and Pakistan conducted, the issue of Kashmir has been internationalized to some extent. That could be a good thing, though not if the U.S. acts as a unilateral superpower and takes it upon itself to impose a "solution." Before you would not discuss human rights violations in Kashmir. There were only these militants who were shot in encounters, Pakistani terrorists and so on. That has changed.

Now with the elections, the dislodging of Farooq Abdullah, and Mufti Muhammad Sayeed coming in, I sense a slight break in the refusal to admit what is really happening in Kashmir.[17] I hear people asking questions

85

about the status of Kashmir. I hear more people saying that maybe Kashmiris should be consulted, instead of this being made to seem like an issue between India and Pakistan.

The first step toward a solution would be for India and Pakistan to open up the borders, to allow people to come and go. If you think of the world as a global village, a fight between India and Pakistan is like a fight between the poorest people in the poorest quarters—the Adivasis and the Dalits. And in the meantime, the zamindars are laying the oil pipelines and selling both parties weapons.

You're from the southwest of India, Kerala, and now you're living in the north. Language, music, food—there's a completely different vibration between the north and the south. Also it seems that the communal tensions in the south are much less than in the north. Am I misreading that?

Kerala has the highest number of RSS cells now. But so far, you're absolutely right. The BJP just haven't even managed to get a toe-hold in the electoral political scene, but they are very hard at work. The first time I ever saw an RSS march—with all these men in khaki shorts—was this year in Kerala, when I went to court. I was just shocked to see them marching in the gloom. It put a chill into my heart.

Talk a little bit about the print media.

The difference between Indian newspapers and newspapers that you'd see in America or England or Europe is the number of stories that there are about politics and politicians. Almost too many. Politicians keep us busy with their shenanigans and eventually every single issue, whether it's a caste massacre in Bihar or communal violence in Gujarat or the issue of displacement by dams, is turned into a noisy debate about whether the Chief Minister should resign or not. The issue itself is never followed up. The murderers are never punished.

If you know anything about a particular issue, if you know the facts and the figures, you see how shockingly wrong newspapers always are. It's quite sad, the lack of discipline in terms of just getting it right, the lack of rigor. The encouraging thing is that there is a tradition of little magazines, community newspapers, pamphlets—an anarchic network of maverick publications, which makes the media hard to control. The big English national dailies don't reach the mass of the people in India. They don't matter as much as they imagine they do. But let's say there's a war against Pakistan or somebody, everybody just becomes jingoistic and nationalistic, just like what happens in the United States. It's no different.

BJP leader L.K. Advani is one of the most powerful members of the government. He took issue with Amartya Sen, the Nobel Prize–winner in economics, on the issue of economics and India.[18]

He said that it was much more important for India to have weapons than to educate people.

Education and health was not the answer for India's development. It was defense.

Advani is the hard core of the center—though today I was delighted to read on the front page of the papers that Advani has been denounced by the Vishwa Hindu Parishad as a pseudo-secularist. "Pseudo-secularist" was a term that Advani had coined to dismiss all those who were not communal fascists, and for him to have his own coinage used against him is delightful.[19]

The Sangh Parivar—the Hindu right-wing family of parties, cultural guilds, the Hindutva lot—squabble with each other in public in order to make everybody feel they're at loggerheads. At the end of it all, Vajpayee keeps the moderates happy, Advani keeps the hard-liners happy, the VHP and the Bajrang Dal keep the rabid

88

fringe happy. Everybody thinks they actually have differences, but the differences are just short of being serious. It's like a traveling, hydra-headed circus. It's like a Hindi movie. It has everything: sex, violence, pathos, humor, comedy, tragedy. Full value for the money. You go home satiated.

India Today, *a weekly magazine, has a fairly large circulation. It recently had a cover story entitled "India Is Now the Electronic Housekeeper of the World."*[20] *General Electric, American Express, Citibank, AT&T, and other U.S. corporations are shifting what they call their back-office operations to India. It's called the fastest-growing industry in India, and the workers are mostly young women. Many are hired to answer customer service questions for U.S. customers. They might be on the other end of the line when I want someone to look up the balance on my credit card account or when Avis telemarkets a cheap vacation package to San Diego. They take on American names and American personas, and tell jokes in American English. The people who are in favor of corporate globalization say this is a great thing. These girls would not ordinarily get jobs, and now they have an opportunity to earn some money. Is there anything wrong with that argument?*

The call center industry is based on lies and racism. The people who call in are being misled into believing

Arundhati Roy and David Barsamian

that they are talking to some white American sitting in America. The people who work in those call centers are told that they're not good enough for the market, that U.S. customers will complain if they find out that their service is being provided by an Indian. So Indians must take on false identities, pretend to be Americans, learn a "correct" accent. It leads to psychosis.

One way of looking at this is to say, "These people at least have jobs." You could say that about prostitution or child labor or anything—"At least they're being paid for it." Their premise is that either these workers don't have jobs or they have jobs in which they have to humiliate themselves. But is that the only choice? That's the question.

We hear all this talk about integrating the world economically, but there is an argument to be made for *not* integrating the world economically. Because what is corporate globalization? It isn't as if the entire world is intermeshed with each other. It's not like India and Thailand or India and Korea or India and Turkey are connected. It's more like America is the hub of this huge cultural and economic airline system. It's the nodal point.

90

The Checkbook and the Cruise Missile

Everyone has to be connected through America, and to some extent Europe.

When powers at the hub of the global economy decide that you have to be X or Y, then if you're part of that network, you have to do it. You don't have the independence of being nonaligned in some way, politically or culturally or economically. If America goes down, then everybody goes down. If tomorrow the United States decides that it wants these call center jobs back, then overnight this billion-dollar industry will collapse in India. It's important for countries to develop a certain degree of economic self-sufficiency. Just in a theoretical sense, it's important for everybody not to have their arms wrapped around each other or their fingers wrapped around each others' throats at all times, in all kinds of ways.

There's a lot of talk about terrorism. In fact, it's become almost an obsession for the media in the United States. But it's a very narrow definition of terrorism..

Yes. It completely ignores the economic terrorism unleashed by neoliberalism, which devastates the lives of millions of people, depriving them of water, food, electricity. Denying them medicine. Denying them education. Terrorism is the logical extension of this business of the free market. Terrorism is the privatization of war. Terrorists are the free marketeers of war—people who believe that it isn't only the state that can wage war, but private parties as well.

If you look at the logic underlying an act of terrorism and the logic underlying a retaliatory war against terrorism, they are the same. Both terrorists and governments make ordinary people pay for the actions of their governments. Osama bin Laden is making people pay for the actions of the U.S. state, whether it's in Saudi Arabia, Palestine, or Afghanistan. The U.S. government is making the people of Iraq pay for the actions of Saddam Hussein. The people of Afghanistan pay for the crimes of the Taliban. The logic is the same.

Osama bin Laden and George Bush are both terrorists. They are both building international networks that perpetrate terror and devastate people's lives. Bush, with the Pentagon, the WTO, the IMF, and the World Bank. Bin Laden with Al Qaeda. The difference is that nobody elected bin Laden. Bush was elected (in a manner of speaking), so U.S. citizens are more responsible for his actions than Iraqis are for the actions of Saddam Hussein or Afghans are for the Taliban. And yet hundreds of thousands of Iraqis and Afghans have been killed, either by economic sanctions or cruise missiles, and we're told that these deaths are the result of "just wars." If there is such a thing as a just war, who is to decide what is just and what is not? Whose God is going to decide that?

The United States has only three or four percent of the world's population, yet it's consuming about a third of the world's natural resources, and to maintain that kind of disparity and imbalance requires force, the use of violence.

The U.S. solution to the spiralling inequalities in the world is not to search for a more equal world, or a way of making things more egalitarian, but to espouse the doctrine of "full-spectrum dominance." The U.S. government is now speaking about putting down unrest from space.[21] It's a terrorist state, and it is laying out a legitimate blueprint for state-sponsored terrorism.

Do you find the persistence of romantic images of India in the West—that this is a country of sitar players and yogis and people who meditate, who are in a kind of ethereal zone? Are those clichés still pretty alive and active?

All clichés are structured around a grain of truth, but there are other clichés now, too. I think that the BJP's few years in power have given an ugly edge to India's image

93

internationally. What happened in Gujarat—the pogrom against the Muslim community—has also become a part of the image of what India is: complex, difficult to understand, full of anachronisms and contradictions, and so on. People from India are in the center of a lot of the intellectual debate about where the world is headed. I think the anarchy of Indian civil society is an important example in the world today, even though India has its back against the wall, and is being bullied and bludgeoned by the WTO and the IMF, and by our own corrupt politicians.

I was in Italy last month at a film festival, and there were documentary films being screened about the Narmada and about other human rights issues. The whole Italian press had gathered. Journalists were expecting me to talk about how terrible things are in India. I did talk about that. But I said, "We're not yet in such a bad way that we have a prime minister who owns six television channels and three newspapers and all the publishing houses and the retail outlets and the book shops. And at least when I'm taken to prison, I know that I'm taken to prison. I know that physically my body is being put in prison. It's not like my mind has been indoctrinated to the point that I *think* I'm free when I'm not."

The Checkbook and the Cruise Missile

In India, we are fighting to retain a wilderness that we have. Whereas in the West, it's gone. Every person that's walking down the street is a walking bar code. You can tell where their clothes are from, how much they cost, which designer made which shoe, which shop you bought each item from. Everything is civilized and tagged and valued and numbered and put in its place. Whereas in India, the wilderness still exists—the unindoctrinated wilderness of the mind, full of untold secrets and wild imaginings. It's threatened, but we're fighting to retain it. We don't have to reconjure it. It's there. It's with us. It's not got signposts all the way. There is that space that hasn't been completely mapped and taken over and tagged and trademarked. I think that's important. And it's important that in India, we understand that it's there and we value it.

Just from hearing you speak and the expression on your face, which I wish people could see, it's obvious that you care a lot about this country. You have a deep affection for it.

I'm not a patriot. I'm not somebody who says, "I love India," and waves a flag around in my head. It's my place. I'm used to it. When people talk about reclaiming the commons, I keep saying, "No, reclaim the wilderness."

95

Not reclaim it, but claim it, hold onto it. It's for that reason that I cannot see myself living away from India. As a
writer, it's where I mess around. Every day, I'm taken by
surprise by something.

I don't know if I'm making myself clear. There is just
a space for the unpredictable here, which is life as it
should be. It's not always that the unpredictable is wonderful—most of the time it isn't. Most of the time it's
brutal and it's terrible. Even when it comes to my work
and myself, I'm ripped apart here. I'm called names. I'm
insulted. But it's the stuff of life. The subjects I write
about raise these huge passions. It's why I keep saying,
"What's dissent without a few good insults?" [22] You have
to be able to take that. If they call you names, you have to
just smile and know that you've touched a nerve.

The point is that we have to rescue democracy by being troublesome, by asking questions, by making a noise.
That's what you have to do to retain your freedoms. Even
if you lose. Even if the NBA loses the battle against the
Sardar Sarovar, it has demonstrated the absolute horrors
of what it means to displace people, what it means to
build a big dam. It's asked these questions. It hasn't gone

quietly. That's the important thing. It's important not to just look at it in terms of winning and losing.

If you look at it another way, look at what we're managing to achieve. We're putting so much pressure that the other side is having to strip. It's having to show itself naked in all its brutality. It's having to drop its masks, its disguises, and reveal its raw and crude and brutal nature. And that's a victory. Not just in terms of who's winning and who's losing, because I'm the kind of person who will always be on the losing side by definition. I have to be, because I'm on this side of the line. I'll never be on that side of the line.

Many journalists have come to you, the BBC, Deutsche Welle. What is interesting for you in these interviews? They must have the same questions, like "When are you going to write another novel?"

I'm the kind of person who sharpens my thinking in public. It could be in an interview or at a lecture. I like talking to strangers. I like talking to people who have read my work. It's a process of thinking aloud. It's not just journalists that ask you the same question. In our lives, whether you're famous or not famous, there's so much repetition, and it's not a terrible thing. If you look at every person you're talking to as a human being, and you're having a conversation with them, then it's never boring. It's only if you're not interested in that person and you're only interested in yourself that it becomes boring. Then you start reciting what amounts to press handouts, which would be terrible.

I'm not necessarily the kind of writer who holes up somewhere and then emerges. I did that with my novel. I don't talk when I'm writing fiction. It's a very private act. But in my political work, I think aloud. I like to pit my mind against another person's, or think together with people. It's not necessarily just with journalists, or interviewers with whom I work. It's an interesting process.

There's a great historic figure in American history, the African-American abolitionist Frederick Douglass. He once said that "[p]ower concedes nothing without a demand. It never did and it never will."[23]

In India, very often, people—not just the government, but people—say, "Oh look, we're so much better off than, say, people in Afghanistan or people in Nepal or people in Pakistan." Somehow they seem to suggest that this has to do with the fact that our government is not as violent as the governments in these other countries. But I think it's because the people are more anarchic, in the sense that it is because we are a troublesome people, a troublesome constituency. And that is why it's difficult to imagine India under army rule. It's unthinkable that Indian society would defer to the army like it does in Pakistan. Even if resistance movements like the movement in the Narmada valley don't succeed in their ultimate goal of stopping a particular dam or "development" project, they do create a spirit among exploited, oppressed people: "You can't do this to us. And if you do, we're going to be extremely troublesome about it."

There were a lot of people who were very annoyed with me when I criticized the Supreme Court and I refused to apologize. But you have to ask these public questions. The minute you start giving ground, you're on a slippery slope.

If you put your ear to the ground in this part of the world today, what do you hear?

Communal talk. Talk about religious identity, ethnic identity, tribal identity. Economically, as globalization is pushed down our throats, people are fractured into tribal, communal groups. The world is getting more and more fractured. Nationalism, nuclearism, communalism, fascism, these things are springing up.

99

Arundhati Roy and David Barsamian

There's always been tension between the majority commu-
nity—the Hindus in India—and the large Muslim minority. But
you are clearly seeing an increase in that tension.

There was a terrible episode of bloodshed and massacre and mayhem during the Partition. About a million
people were massacred. The wounds of that were never
allowed to heal by the Congress Party, which harnessed
this hatred and used it to play electoral games. Our kind
of electoral democracy seems to demand the breaking up
of the electorate into vote banks. But today all the things
that the Congress Party did at night, the BJP and its Sangh
Parivar does in the daytime. They do it with pride, as policy. Now they're in power, they're in government, they
have penetrated every state organ. Whether it's rewriting
the history books, or placing their people in the bureaucracy, in the police, in the army. Of course, when the
Congress Party was in power, it was their people. But
their people were not self-professedly communal people.
They did it as a sly, undercover game.

In the past, historians or politicians or bureaucrats
would not openly say that India is a Hindu country. But
now nobody is shy about saying this. The RSS now has
thousands of branches all over the country. They have

funds, they have means, they have resources to indoctrinate young minds. Once you inject this poison into the bloodstream, it's very hard to work it out of the system. So now the fact is, whether the BJP wins the next elections or not, their agenda is on the table. The country has been militarized and communalized and nuclearized. The Congress has no means to deal with it. It hasn't been able to counter that in any moral or political way.

Let's say you want to write about a particular topic that interests you. First of all, how do you make that selection, and then how do you go about researching it?

You should never ask me these method questions, because there's never any method! It's not as though I cold-bloodedly go out and select some topic for academic or career reasons. In the case of the nuclear tests, the nuclear tests happened while I was in the United States. My first reaction was one of rage at the hypocrisy there: "The blacks can't manage the bomb." Then I came back here and saw the shrill jingoism. So I wrote "The End of Imagination." When you start getting into the debate about national security, every country can justify having nuclear weapons. I think it's very important not to enter the debate on their terms, on the terms that the army and the politicians and the bureaucracy would like to set. Because every country can have a pragmatic *realpolitik* justification for why it needs nuclear weapons.

In the case of the Narmada, it was more something that I really had for years wanted to understand. In February 1999, the Supreme Court lifted its stay on the building of the Sardar Sarovar Dam. Suddenly it looked as if this battle, which many of us on the outside of this movement had thought was being won, had been dealt a body blow. I started reading. I went to the valley, I met the activists, and felt that the movement needed to tell its story in a way which is accessible to an ordinary reader. It needed a novelist's skill. It's a complex issue, and much of the time the establishment depends on the fact that people don't understand. I wanted to build a narrative that could puncture that—to deal with all their arguments, to deal with their facts and figures, to counter them in a way ordinary people could understand.

One thing leads to another. If you read all the political essays, each one dovetails into the next. Going to the Narmada valley, you see that the fight against the Sardar Sarovar, which is a state-built dam, is different from the fight against the Maheshwar Dam, which was the first privatized project in India. Then you start asking these questions about the privatization of infrastructure and it leads you to the whole question of privatization and what is going on there. So that led to my essay "Power Politics."

It is interesting to see how the establishment deals with dissent. It gives you a fair idea of who the establishment really is. You see who crawls out of the woodwork to take you on. Very often, it's an unexpected person. It's not the people who are completely on the other side of the spectrum, who are completely opposed to your point of view. It will be cowardly people who position themselves as being "balanced" critics. They really can't deal with the real questions, because they're instinctively undemocratic. There is nothing they condemn more passionately than passion. But I insist on the right to be emotional, to be sentimental, to be passionate. If displacement, dispossession, killing, and injustice on the scale that takes place in India does not enrage us, what will?

When people try to dismiss those who ask the big public questions as being emotional, it is a strategy to avoid debate. Why should we be scared of being angry? Why should we be scared of our feelings, if they're based

on facts? The whole framework of reason versus passion
is ridiculous, because often passion is based on reason.
Passion is not always unreasonable. Anger is based on
reason. They're not two different things. I feel it's very
important to defend that. To defend the space for feelings, for emotions, for passion. I'm often accused of the
crime of having feelings. But I'm not pretending to be a
"neutral" academic. I'm a writer. I have a point of view. I
have feelings about the things I write about—and I'm going to express them.

*That reminds me of a famous Urdu couplet by Muhammad
Iqbal: "Love leaped into Nimrod's fire without hesitation. / Mean-
while, reason is on the rooftop, just comtemplating the scene."*[24]
There is that kind of juxtaposition of the intellect versus feeling.

I think the opposite. I think that my passion comes
from my intellect. So much of the way I love comes from
the way I think. Thinking makes great loving. I don't acknowledge this artificial boundary between the intellect
and the heart. They're not as separate as literature and poetry makes them out to be. Their fusion is what makes
artists and writers. I believe in succumbing to the beauty
of feelings, and I believe in the rigor of the intellect, too. I

don't believe in over ripe passion. But I believe that there isn't anything as wonderful as a fierce intellectual passion.

Do you ever experience writer's block, where you have real diffi-culty in writing? Do you have any techniques to get out of it? Do you exercise or walk around the block or eat oranges?

No. I haven't gone through that. Not yet. I don't look at writing as a profession, a career. If I can't write, I won't write. I'll do something else. It's important to understand that one is not that significant. It doesn't matter. If you can do something, great; if you can't do it, it's okay.

Often I tell myself, "Don't do it. Don't write." Because I don't want to enter an arena that I know will consume my soul. I don't want to take on Narendra Modi or write about the riots in Gujarat. But, it's very hard to keep quiet. This hammering sets up in my head. My non-fiction is wrenched out of me. It's written when I don't want to write. So when people say, "You're very brave" or "You're very courageous," I feel a bit embar-rassed. Because it isn't bravery or courage. I have to do it. Often I don't want to see or understand. But I can't not, because the story clamors to be told and then I'm just the go-between that sits down and tells it, in some way.

What advice would you give to people, in terms of thinking out-side the box, outside of what's called conventional wisdom, for example?

I'm very bad at giving advice!

For yourself, then, how do you do it? And how did you develop it, because it's something that's acquired. It's not necessarily innate, like a sense of smell.

I wonder. I didn't grow up within a conventional kind of family and I wasn't in a city. I was this child who was wandering all over the place, spending hours on the river alone, fishing. My childhood's greatest gift was a lack of indoctrination. So it's not that I'm somebody's who's re-markable because I've learned to think outside the box. The fact is that the box was never imposed on me. I never went to a formal school until I was about ten. There was a delightful absence of a box.

We were in a way very cosmopolitan and in a way completely local and rural. It's an odd combination. I always had trouble if anyone asked me the most normal questions, like, "Where are you from, what's your name, what's your mother tongue, what does your father do?" I had no answers for any of these questions, because I just didn't know my father and it was difficult to explain the complexities of my childhood. But if you asked me completely unconventional questions, then I could answer them, because I would think about them. These normal things were not easy for me to reply to.

As you've grown older, have you gotten an opportunity to know your father?

I've met him. Yes. At least I know what he looks like.

I was at Delhi University a few days ago, and a student asked me, "What would you do in a public sector that is inefficient and has an overbloated bureaucracy and is losing money?" What's wrong with privatizing that?

People in India especially, but in the third world generally, are being made to believe that this is the only choice. You have a choice between a corrupt public sector and an efficient private sector. If those are the only two options, anyone would say, "I'll have the efficient private sector." In fact, many of the public sector units that are being privatized were actually profit-making. For instance, Bharat Heavy Electricals, which manufactures turbines and heavy electrical machinery, was one of the foremost manufacturers in the world. As soon as the government decided to privatize it about ten years ago, they deliberately allowed everything to go to seed, and then they said, "Look, isn't it terrible?" It's propaganda, this opposition of the sleek, efficient private sector and the corrupt, terrible government. Of course, the public power sector has been incredibly corrupt and inefficient. The transmission and distribution losses have been tremendous. But what does the government do? It signs up with Enron. What is happening with Enron today? The government is paying Enron not to produce electricity, because it's so expensive.

So Enron, even though it's bankrupt in the United States and disgraced, is still sucking money out of the Indian economy?

There's a big litigation process on, but, yes, that's the situation.

Bill Gates of Microsoft, one of the sahibs of the new world economic order, was shopping in Delhi last week. He met with top government officials and CEOs. You saw something very interesting on TV about how Indians view Gates.

I was watching some music channel—not MTV, but some other music channel—this morning. On the screen it said, "What does Bill Gates really want?" Then they had interviews with maybe twenty young students. Every single one of them said he's here to blow open the market for Windows and he's just trying to get publicity by giving money for AIDS. Nobody was under any illusions about what his visit was about.

Does that encourage you, that people have that understanding?

Three or four months ago, I went to a seminar on the power sector, and I thought to myself, "What are you doing here? How can you be sitting in this seminar on the privatization of power?" If someone had told me four years ago that I would be attending meetings about electricity, I would have laughed. But it was uplifting to listen to the kind of minds that are at work here. People can just take the whole thing apart and critique it. The first critique of the Power Purchase Agreement with Enron came from a small NGO in Pune, called Prayas.[25] Everything they said has come true. That is a great thing about India. There is a very strong intellectual ability to take something apart, in a way that I really appreciate and admire.

To what extent do you think that the British used "divide and rule" as a strategy to maintain control of India—a vast country? The British had very few soldiers and administrators here.

The British certainly used divide-and-rule tactics, but the British empire survived because it coopted the Indian elite. It's the same technique that empire uses now to propagate its neoliberal reign.

Have you read the work of Martin Luther King, Jr.? He was influenced by Gandhi. People in the United States generally know about his "I Have a Dream" speech from the 1963 March on Washington, but not a lot of Americans know about the speech he gave in New York in 1967 at Riverside Church. He became increasingly radical later in his life, and in New York he said, "True compassion is more than flinging a coin to a beggar. It comes to see that an edifice which produces beggars needs restructuring." [26]

That is the terrible dilemma of living in India, isn't it? Every moment of every day, you're faced with the brutal inequalities of the society you live in. So it is impossible to forget, even for a moment. Just to enjoy the ordinary daily things—the clothes you wear, the fun you have, the music you listen to, the roof over your head, the meal in the evening—involves knowing that other people don't have these privileges.

We have been taught that peace is the opposite of war. But is it? In India, peace is a daily battle for food and shelter and dignity.

The Checkbook and the Cruise Missile

Martin Luther King, Jr. wrote in his "Letter from Birmingham Jail," that true peace is not merely "the absence of tension" but "the presence of justice." [27]

Or at least the journey toward justice, toward some vision of egalitarianism. Which is what I think is fundamentally the problem with the whole ethic of neoliberal neo-capitalism. You make it all right to grab. You say that it's all right to get ahead by hitting the next person on the head. It's all right to accumulate capital and profits at someone else's expense. It destroys the fabric of concern and fellow-feeling. There is a finite amount of capital in the world, and if you accumulate, you're grabbing from somebody. That's not right.

Another of the sahibs who recently has been in Delhi is Paul O'Neill, the U.S. Treasury Secretary. He was talking on November 22 to an audience of corporate leaders, and he was very critical of India, a country, he said, where "corruption and bribery are widespread, frightening away honest businessmen and investors." [28]

If it's frightening away investors like Enron and Bechtel, it can only be a good thing.

It's interesting that he should be lecturing Indians about corruption and bribery, because the United States has just gone through what Business Week *calls the most unprecedented "corporate*

111

crime wave" in its history.[29] *Not just Enron, but WorldCom, Xerox, Tyco, Arthur Andersen—a huge number of corporations have been guilty of insider trading and all kinds of shenanigans.*

When have America's own shortcomings prevented it from lecturing to other people? That's par for the course.

Howard Zinn, the great American historian, said there was the Bronze Age, the Iron Age, and today we live in the Age of Irony.[30]

Irony is a kind word for the crimes of the American empire.

In your essay entitled "Come September," you are very critical of U.S. policy in support of Israel and its repression of the Palestinians. You must know that this is a hot-button issue in the United States. It's difficult to talk about Israel critically without immediately being labeled in the most unflattering terms. Why did you choose to talk about this?

I was talking about the eleventh of September, and I thought I should remind people that the eleventh of September 1922 was when imperial Britain marked out a mandate on Palestine, after the Balfour Declaration. Eighty years on, the Palestinians are still under siege. How can one come to the United States and not mention Israel's illegal occupation of Palestinian territory? The U.S.

government is funding it and supporting it politically and morally. It's a crime.

Diaspora communities are notorious for having very inflammatory views. If you look at the most right-wing, unreasonable, vituperative Hindus, many live in the United States. Every time you get a letter to the editor saying, "I think there should be nuclear war and Pakistan should be destroyed," it will be somebody who lives in Champaign-Urbana or some other U.S. town. I've never been to Israel, but I've been told that in Israel the media reflects a broader spectrum of opinion than you see in the United States.

What do you think of the report that just came out looking at the Indian diaspora community in the United States? Apparently, some segments of it are sending a lot of money to support Hindu fundamentalist organizations.[31]

The report seems quite credible. It's quite important that this kind of dogged work in being done. It's really wonderful. These groups hide behind the fact that they do charity work, though their charity is all about the Hinduization of tribal people. But in India, these things will not be investigated.

Arundhati Roy and David Barsamian

*What was your take on the U.S. presidential election in the
year 2000, especially in light of the U.S. tendency to be very critical of
how elections are conducted in other countries.*

I have to say that I didn't follow it very closely, because if you don't live in America, whether it's Bush or
Clinton or Gore, it doesn't seem to make that much difference. I personally feel that if the September 11 attacks
had happened when Clinton was in power, it could have
been worse for the world in a way, because he at least
doesn't sound as stupid as Bush. Bush is vicious but he's
comical. He's easy meat. Whereas Clinton is far cleverer
and more calculating. He's more of a show man. I don't
think there's much to choose between them.

*You have used the word "bully" to describe the United States
and its policies. I think maybe some Americans might have difficulty
identifying their state as a bully because of a lack of information
about what's going on outside.*

People from poorer places and poorer countries have
to call upon their compassion not to be angry with ordinary people in America. I certainly do. Every time I write
something, that anger does come out, and then I pull it
back, because I tell myself, "They don't know. These are
people who don't know what is being done in their

name." Yet, I keep wondering if that's because it suits them not to know. I have to remind myself about the extent of the brainwashing that goes on there. But I think that if most people knew what was being done in their names, they would be mortified. The question is: how do we let them know?

Ben Bagdikian and others have written extensively about how the corporate media operates in the United States, and by extension in the rest of the world because of its enormous reach.[32] Do you think that the people who work for these corporations know the reality, know the facts about what's going on and are repressing it? Or are they truly ignorant?

I'm sure the senior people know. The junior people are sent on a beat and told to cover something and they cover it. So I don't think everybody knows the key secret and is suppressing it. Journalists have the illusion of independence. But certainly the people who make the decisions know.

Where are the spaces for dissidents in the Indian context? What about television?

There's no space on TV whatsoever. Not even to show a documentary film, like, say, Sanjay Kak's film on the Narmada. We don't even begin to think that it will be shown on TV.

Why not? Why isn't there a station or a network?

Why not? You can't even have a private screening of a documentary film without a censor certificate. When Anand Patwardhan made his documentary about the nuclear issue, the censor board told him, "You can't show politicians in your film." *You can't show politicians in your film!* What does that mean? You can't have politicians making political speeches in your film![33] It's really Kafkaesque. Yet they can't police everything. It's too difficult.

In a country like the United States where books like Chomsky's *9–11* are starting to reach wider audiences, aren't people going to feel a bit pissed off that they had no idea about what was going on, and what was being done in their name?[34] If the corporate media continues to be as outrageous in its suppression of facts as it is, it might just lift off like a scab. It might become something that's totally irrelevant, that people just don't believe. Because, ultimately, people are interested in their own safety.

The policies the U.S. government is following are dangerous for its citizens. It's true that you can bomb or buy out anybody that you want to, but you can't control the rage that's building in the world. You just can't. And that rage will express itself in some way or the other. Condemning violence is not going to be enough. How can you condemn violence when a section of your economy is based on selling weapons and making bombs and piling up chemical and biological weapons? When the soul of your culture worships violence? On what grounds are you going to condemn terrorism, unless you change your attitude toward violence?

With very few exceptions, the September 11 attacks are presented as actions by people who simply hate America. It's separated from any political background. That has confused a lot of people.

It was a successful strategy, this isolation of the events of September 11 from history, insisting that terrorism is an evil impulse with no context. The minute you try and put it into a context, you are accused of excusing it or justifying it. It's like telling a scientist who is researching drugs for malaria that he or she is in cahoots with the female anopheles mosquito. If you're trying to understand something, it doesn't mean you're justifying it. The fact is, if you can justify all the wars that you have fought, all the murders that you've committed, all the countries that you've bombed, all the ecologies that you've destroyed, if you can justify that, then Osama bin Laden can certainly use the same logic to justify September 11. You can't have a political context for one kind of terrorism and no political context for another.

So if you were to talk to an average American, what would be something that you would say, in terms of trying to understand why there is animosity toward the United States, why there is rage and anger?

I was in America in September 2002, as you know. I was very reluctant to come. I thought there just wasn't any point in saying these things, because I don't believe in "speaking truth to power." I don't believe that there is any way in which you can persuade that kind of power to act differently unless it's in its own self-interest. There isn't any point. But my editor, Anthony Arnove, persuaded me to come, and I'm so glad that I did, because it was very, very nice for me to see how human and open the people I met were. People were clearly trying to understand what was going on in the world. It was an important trip for me.

I had exactly the opposite experience from what I expected. I had people coming up to me on the street saying, "Thank you for saying what you said" and "We can't say it because we're so scared, but thank you." It was wonderful for me that it happened. It made me believe that the reason that so much energy and money is poured into manipulating the media is because the establishment fears public opinion. They know that ordinary people are not as ruthless, as cold, as calculating, as powerful people.

Ordinary people do have a conscience. Ordinary people don't necessarily always act in their own selfish interests. If the bubble were to burst, and people were to know all of the horrendous things that have been carried out in their name, I think it would go badly for the American establishment. And I think it has begun. I think all America's family secrets are spilling out backstage on the Green Room floor. I really think so. Yes, it's true that the corporate media just blanks out everything, but on the Internet, some of the most outraged, incandescently angry pieces are written by Americans. A film like "Bowling for Columbine" has been shown everywhere and it connects the dots in ways which ordinary people can understand. This is important. I think it's beginning to unravel, actually. I think the propaganda machine is going to come apart.

Arundhati Roy and David Barsamian

What about the role of intellectuals in the propaganda machine? In the United States, intellectuals are supposed to be neutral. They're supposed to accumulate facts and present them without presuming to be on one side or the other. They're encouraged to use obscure jargon. For example, there are no ideas—everything is a "notion." No one talks, it's all "discourse." It's what we call pomo, postmodernism. Do you have something like that in India?

We have pomo in India, too. Definitely. A lot of it has to do with the sad business of creating a little expertise, so that you come off sounding special, as if the world couldn't do without you. A little hunk of expertise that you can carry off to your lair and guard against the unauthorized curiosity of passers-by. My enterprise is the opposite: to never complicate what is simple, to never simplify what is complicated. But I think it's very important to be able to communicate to ordinary people what is happening in the world. There's a whole industry working hard at trying to prevent people from understanding what is being done to them.

Chomsky calls them a mandarin class of specialists.

Experts take away the ability to make decisions from people. In courts, language has evolved in such a way that ordinary people simply can't understand. You have this phalanx of lawyers and judges who are deciding vitally important issues, but people can't understand what is being said, what the procedure really is, what's going on.

I noticed that in the film "DAM/AGE," it was difficult to follow some of the pronouncements from the Supreme Court.

"Vicious stultification and vulgar debunking cannot be allowed to pollute the stream of justice" [laughs]. What is the other one? "Contumacious violation…" I've forgotten. I used to know it by heart.

Do you see any role for specialized knowledge?

I see a role for specialized knowledge, but I think that it's important for there to be an arena where it is shared, where it is communicated. It's not that somebody shouldn't have specialized knowledge. The ability to dig a trench and lay a cable is a kind of specialized knowledge. Farmers have specialized knowledge, too. The question is: what sort of knowledge is privileged in our societies? I don't think that a CEO is more valuable to society and ought to be paid ten million dollars a year, while farmers and laborers starve.

The range of what is valued has become so extreme that one lot of people have captured it and left three-quarters of the world to live in unthinkable poverty, because their work is not valued. What would happen if the sweepers of the city went on strike or the sewage system didn't work? A CEO wouldn't be able to deal with his own shit.

Macaulay, a Raj official in the nineteenth century, imperiously declared that "a single shelf of a good European library [is] worth the whole native literature of India and Arabia." [35] *In recent years there's been an enormous surge of writing produced not only by Indian writers such as yourself but also writers of Indian origin who live outside of India, like V.S. Naipaul? Why is that happening now?*

It's not that enormous a surge, actually. I remember when my novel was first published, *The New Yorker* organized to shoot one big photograph of Indo-Anglian writers.[36] There were maybe ten or fifteen of us. They'd organized this huge bus to take us to lunch, and the bus was empty. Everyone's talking about this surge but you can count the people who are known on your fingertips. It's being made out to be something more than it is, I think.

Like a fad?

There are people writing, but it's not some renaissance or anything that's happening. If it is a fad for the Western world, then that's their business. I don't care.

The Checkbook and the Cruise Missile

Some people might say that writing in English automatically means you're writing for a yuppie audience, because English in India particularly is a language of privilege.

That's true. But at the same time, any language in India is very limited. If you write in Malayalam, only someone from Kerala can read it. If you write in Hindi, only those from a few states in the North can read it. So language is a very complicated issue in India. It's interesting that *The God of Small Things* has been published in forty languages, so in a way it's about language, but not as in English or German or French or Hindi. It's something more than that. It's language as communication, more or less.

My political writing is published in many, many Indian languages. The Hindi translation of *The God of Small Things* is almost ready. So it's no longer just for yuppies. And anyway it's not just yuppies who speak English in India. There are more people who speak English in India than in England. It's a huge number.

One of the pleasures for me about having written *The God of Small Things* is that many of the people who are reading it would not normally read an English novel. So a sub-inspector from Muzaffarnagar or some person from some village somewhere will come to me and say, "I read it with a dictionary. I understood it." So I love the range of readers—from John Updike to a policeman in Muzaffarnagar.

Your articles and essays appear in The Nation *magazine, and you're publishing now with South End Press.* Power Politics *is your first book with them and* War Talk *is the next one. Are you getting a lot of response from outside India? Are people writing to you?*

I do receive a lot of letters, but it's difficult for me to deal with the volume of responses and requests that I get. I'm under pressure to turn myself into an institution, to have an office and secretaries and people dealing with my mail and my accounts. I'm just not like that. I can't be like that. So I choose the inefficient model, which is not to deal with it. I do what I can. Obviously I have a literary agent in America and in England. They help me. But in my own space, I just don't have that. It's hard, but it's a choice that I make, that I just continue to be an individual who gets a lot of mail and can't handle it.

Himanshu Thakker is someone whom you admire. You mention him in the introduction to The Cost of Living.[37] *I happened to meet him and he told me, "You know, it's remarkable. The women are the leaders in the country. The women are advancing the movements for social justice." Why is that?*

I don't know but it's absolutely correct. In India, the legacy of the freedom struggle has been a great respect for nonviolent resistance. The pros and cons of violent and nonviolent resistance can be debated, but I don't think there can be any doubt that violent resistance harms women physically and psychologically in deep and complex ways. Having said that, Indian society is still deeply disrespectful of women. The daily violence, injustice, and indignity heaped on women is hard to believe sometimes.

But this takes place against a backdrop of an institutionalized misogyny that is deeply culturally imbedded. One example was a report in The Times of India *a couple of days ago that there's a crisis in Haryana because there are not enough marriageable girls.*[38] *Why aren't there enough marriageable girls? Because of female feticide. The families have to buy brides for their sons from outside the state and their community. It's interesting that the* Times *said that "[d]esperate boys are willing to marry girls from any caste." That's another one of these incredible contradictions.*

That is India. We don't even blink when someone brings up a contradiction. What is interesting is that a lot of the women who are involved in resistance movements and who are activists are also redefining what "modern" means. They are really at war against their community's traditions, on the one hand, and against the kind of modernity that is being imposed by the global economy, on the other. They decide what they want from their own tradition and what they will take from modernity. It's a high-wire act. Very tiring but exhilarating.

Another thing everyone probably has to deal with here is the persistence of color, the emphasis on being fair skinned. I was reading about Kareena Kapoor, a rising young Bollywood starlet (who is opening, incidentally, a Pizza Hut in Gurgaon), and she was described as "cream colored." It's a very favorable designation.

I'm so glad that you brought this up, because most people, foreigners, don't even notice that there's a color difference between white Indians and black Indians. But it's something that really drives me crazy here. India is one of the most racist modern societies. The kind of things people will say about being black-skinned are stunning.

There was a television program a few years ago about this. In the audience there was a Sudanese man, an albino man, and a Punjabi woman who runs a marriage bureau. I've never seen anything more ridiculous. The Sudanese man talked about how terrible it was for him to live here, and how girls would cross to the other side of the road. How people would pull his hair on the bus and call him *hubshi*, which is roughly equivalent to "nigger." Then the albino said, "I don't know whether I would be considered fair or dark." So he asked the woman who runs the marriage bureau whether she could get him a bride. She looked at him and said, "I can get you a polio victim."

This was all being done without irony. At the end of it, the man who was presenting the show said, "It looks like all of us are very color-conscious. In actual fact, why do we spend so much time thinking about the packaging? Black people are also nice from underneath."

If you look at the newspapers, you see advertisements for some cream called Afghan Snow or Fair and Lovely. And all these white women in Bollywood films! Ninety percent of the women in India are black. But, according to Bollywood, if you're not white, you're not beautiful. The rising international popularity of Bollywood films worries me. Most of them reinforce some terrible, some very disempowering values.

Poor people, the Dalits and the Adivasis, are mostly black. There's an apartheid system at work here, for anyone who cares to notice.

Let's go to another Bombay Bollywood star, from an older generation, Nargis. She complained bitterly about Satyajit Ray, the great Indian filmmaker, saying that his films only show poverty. Then she was asked, "Well, what would you rather see in Indian cinema?" And she said "dams."[39]

"You're not showing India in a proper light." That's the great middle-class complaint: "Why can't you show McDonald's and Pizza King?" Because here, you see, people have learned not to see the poverty. They have these filters, these contact lenses, that filter it out. They don't understand why "outsiders" get so exercised about it. They take it as a kind of affront.

I'm interested in how that operates. I've seen it myself, and I see it in myself when I'm here. How do you look away from someone who's terribly poor and indigent?

It's a survival technique. Meaning, how else are you to survive? You have to find a way of continuing with your life. So you just filter it out.

GLOBALIZATION OF DISSENT

In March 2002, a pogrom was carried out against the Muslim population of Gujarat. You've written an essay on this entitled "Democracy: Who Is She When She Is at Home." What happened in Gujarat?

In February 2002, the BJP was gearing up for elections in Uttar Pradesh. They had trundled out their favorite campaign issue, the building of the Ram temple in Ayodhya. Communal tension was at a fever pitch. People were traveling to Ayodhya by train to participate in the building of the temple. At the time, Gujarat was the only major state in India to have a BJP government. It had for some time been the laboratory in which Hindu fascism had been conducting an elaborate experiment. In late

This interview was conducted in Los Angeles, California, on May 26, 2003.

129

February, a train carrying belligerent VHP and Bajrang Dal activists was stopped by a mob outside the Godhra station. A whole compartment of the train was set on fire and fifty-eight people were burnt alive.[1]

Nobody really knew who was responsbile for the carnage. Within hours, a meticulously planned pogrom was unleashed against the Muslim community. About two thousand Muslims were killed. One hundred and fifty thousand were driven from their homes. Women were publicly gang-raped. Parents were bludgeoned to death in front of their children. The leaders of the mob had computer-generated lists marking out Muslim-owned shops, homes, and businesses, which were burned to the ground. Muslim places of worship were desecrated. The mob was equipped with trucks loaded with thousands of gas cylinders that had been horded weeks in advance. The police did not merely protect the mob, but provided covering fire. Within months, Gujarat's Chief Minister, Narendra Modi, announced proudly that he wanted to have early elections. He believed that the pogrom would win him Hindu hearts.

Modi was right, wasn't he?

The Checkbook and the Cruise Missile

Modi's re-election is something that has shaken many of us to the core of our beings. It's one thing to have a dictator who commits genocide. It's another thing to have an elected government with officials who have been accused of actively abetting mass murder being re-elected. Because then all of us must bear the shame of that. All of us must bear some responsibility for that.

But thinking deeply about it, I don't see that it's all that different from the American public electing president after president who has killed and massacred and bombed people all over the world. A child asked me quite recently, "Is Bush better or is Modi better?" I said, "Why are you asking?" He said, "Because Modi killed his own people, and Bush is killing other people." That's how clear children can be. Eventually, after thinking about it, I said, "Well, the people they killed are all people." We have to think like that.

What happened in Gujarat has raised very serious questions. When you speak to somebody and tell them that two thousand Muslims were massacred on the streets of Gujarat, and women were raped, and pregnant women had their stomachs slit open, normal people, or people who are outside that situation, recoil in horror. But people inside that situation say things like, "They deserved it." And how do you deal with that?

It isn't a coincidence that the massacre of Muslims in Gujarat happened after September 11. Gujarat is also one place where the toxic waste of the World Trade Center is being dumped right now.[2] This waste is being being dumped in Gujarat, and then taken off to Ludhiana and places like that to be recycled. I think it's quite a metaphor. The demonization of Muslims has also been given legitimacy by the world's superpower, by the emperor himself. We are at a stage where democracy—this corrupted, scandalous version of democracy—is the problem. So much of what politicians do is with an eye on elections. Wars are fought as election campaigns. In India, Muslims are killed as part of election campaigns. In 1984, after the massacre of Sikhs in Delhi, the Congress Party won, hands down. We must ask ourselves very serious questions about this particular brand of democracy.

What was the response of the political class in India and the media to Modi being re-elected?

The media in India can roughly be divided into the national English media and the local regional language newspapers. Typically, their understandings of similar

132

events are completely different. The local Gujarati press was vehemently anti-Muslim. It manipulated events and supported what was happening. But the English press was very outspoken and condemnatory of what Modi was doing in Gujarat.

It's important to understand that the killing in Gujarat had a long run-up. The climate was created soon after the BJP came to power and India conducted nuclear tests. This whole business of unfettered Hindu nationalism, where else was it going to lead?

The national press supported that idea from the beginning. It supported the Kargil War uncritically. The English-language press in India supports the project of corporate globalization fully. It has no time for dispossession and drought and farmers' debts, the ravages that the corporate globalization project is wreaking on the poor of India. So to suddenly turn around and condemn the riots is a typical middle-class response. Let's support everything that leads to the conditions in which the massacre takes place, but when the killing starts, you recoil in middle-class horror, and say, "Oh, that's not very nice. Can't we be more civilized?"

Arundhati Roy and David Barsamian

Once Modi won the elections, the English-language press began to whip itself and say, "We got it wrong. Maybe the secularists are taking too much of an anti-Hindu position," and rubbish like that. They began to negotiate with the fascists, basically. The Chamber of Indian Industry apologized to Modi for having said things about the fact that genocide was bad for business. They promised to reinvest in Gujarat. So as soon as he won this election, everybody was busy negotiating and retracting. I've lost track of the number of references I've seen in the media to "Modi magic."

What was the response of the so-called intellectual class, academics and writers, to Gujarat and Modi's re-election?

I think everybody felt whipped and beaten, because Modi was gloating. Everybody felt as if they had taken a pounding, which they had, to an extent. I think it threw the opposition—I don't mean the Congress Party when I say the opposition, but the critics of this kind of politics—into disarray, because they felt that, and they were made to feel that, they had no place in modern India. These voices of sanity and reason felt that they had no place.

The Checkbook and the Cruise Missile

Academics have this problem. If you are an economist, you are only an economist. If you are a sociologist, you are only a sociologist. If you are a historian, you're only a historian. And now, to understand what's going on, you must cross disciplines, and you must see the connections between the dispossession and the despair created by corporate globalization, flowing into the bitterness of Partition, flowing into the rhetoric of cultural nationalism. All these things come together to create this situation.

Gujarat is also, ironically, the home state of Mahatma Gandhi. In 1930, there was a very interesting event there. He led a Salt March to the coastal town of Dandi. Why don't you recount that, so people have another kind of historical perspective?

Whatever critique one may or may not have of him, Gandhi's understanding of politics and public imagination is unsurpassed, I would say, by any politician in world history. He knew how to strike at the heart of empire. The Salt March—the Dandi march—when Indians marched to the sea to make salt, was a strike against the salt tax. It wasn't just a symbolic weekend march, but struck at the heart of the economic policies of the colonial regime. What has happened in the evolution of nonviolent resistance is that it's become more and more symbolic, and less and less real. When a symbol unmoors itself from what it symbolizes, it loses meaning. It becomes ineffective.

Fifteen million people marched against the war in Iraq on February 15, 2003, in perhaps the biggest display of public morality ever seen. It was fantastic. But it was symbolic. Governments of today have learned to deal with that. They know to wait out a demonstration or a march. They know the day after tomorrow, opinions can change, or be manipulated into changing. Unless civil disobedience becomes real, not symbolic, there is very little hope for change.

That's a very important lesson that we need to learn from the civil disobedience and the nonviolent resistance of the Indian independence struggle. It was fine political theater, but it was never, ever merely symbolic. It was always a real strike against the economics of imperialism. What was *swadeshi* about? It was saying, "Don't buy British products." It was saying, "Make your own yarn. Make your own salt. We have to take apart the economic machinery of empire now, and strike at it." These marches and songs and meetings of today—they are beautiful, but they are often mostly for us. If all our energies go into organizing these things, then we don't do any real damage to the establishment, to the empire.

There's a lot of talk in the United States now about empire. A new book by British historian Niall Ferguson, Empire, *celebrates the many positive aspects of imperialism, particularly of British rule. The jewel in the crown of Britain, of course, was colonial India.*[3]

It's rather staggering that people like Ferguson are touting the benefits of imperialism. By the middle of the eighteenth century, just about the time that the British took it over, India accounted for nearly twenty-five percent of the world's global trade. When the British left in 1947, this figure had dwindled to around four to five percent. Much scholarly research has demonstrated that during British rule, India's economy underwent a process of peasantization, where urban areas were ruralized, essentially.

Recently, travelling to the West, it's the first time it's even occurred to me that people can actually justify imperialism. Let me say that categorically—politically, socially, economically—there is no justification for colonialism. Next these people will be justifying genocide or slavery. Weren't they the foundations of the American empire?

Do you think that the people of South Africa, or anywhere on the continent of Africa, or India, or Pakistan are longing to be kicked around all over again? Is Ferguson aware of how many million people died in India in the late nineteenth century because of the drought and the famine while food and raw materials were being exported to England? How dare they even talk like this? It's grotesque that anybody can sit down and write a reasoned book on something like this. It is nothing short of grotesque.

Thomas Friedman, the Pulitzer Prize–winning columnist for The New York Times, *has written that "America is in an imperial role here, now. Our security and standing in the world ride on our getting Iraq right."* [4]

Well, it isn't doing it right, is it? But the point is that the justification for going to war against Iraq has been forgotten. The weapons of mass destruction have not been found. You were told in the United States that Iraq was going to annihilate you, just as Cuba was, and Nicaragua was, and El Salvador was, and all the tiny little countries of the world were. After the war, you were told, America was going to be secure. But today, after the war, the terrorist alerts keep being set to purple, or whatever the highest register is. And now you're saying,

The Checkbook and the Cruise Missile

"Al-Qaeda is in Iran, or maybe it's in Syria, or maybe it's in North Korea."

The point is that any kind of justification, any kind of nonsense works because there isn't any real media left in the United States. It's just a kind of propaganda machine that spews out whatever suits the occasion, and banks on people's short memory span.

When you spoke at the World Social Forum in Porto Alegre, Brazil, in late January 2003, you were certain that the United States was going to attack Iraq. In fact, you said, "It's more than clear that Bush is determined to go to war against Iraq, regardless of the facts—and regardless of international public opinion." [5]

I don't think you needed to be a genius to be certain. There is a strategy at work which has nothing to do with the propaganda that's being put out. And when you start to see the pattern, then you have a sense of what is going to happen. After the attack on Afghanistan, you started to see the preparations for the next war against Iraq. And now they are laying the basis for even more wars.

I find it shocking that people should think that world public opinion should have changed because the United States "won" the war. Did anybody think it wasn't going to? Here is a country that is so ruthless in what it is pre-

Arundhati Roy and David Barsamian

pared to do that it's going to win every war that it fights, except if its own people do something about it. There isn't any country that can fight a conventional war against U.S. forces and win.

Talk about how war is viewed as a product to be marketed and sold to the consumers, in this case the American public.

Referring to the timing of the Iraq war, a Bush administration spokesperson said, "From a marketing point of view, you don't introduce new products in August."[6] They were asking themselves, what's the best season to introduce this new product? When should you start the ad campaign? When should you actually launch it? Today, the crossover between Hollywood and the U.S. military is getting more and more promiscuous.

War is also an economic necessity now. A significant section of the U.S. economy depends on the sale of weapons. There has to be a turnover. You can't have cruise missiles lying around on the factory floor. The economies of Europe and the United States depend on the sale and manufacture of weapons. This is a huge imperative to go to war. Apart from this, the United States needs millions of barrels of oil a day to keep its bloated economy chugging along. It needs Iraq. It needs Venezuela.

140

The Checkbook and the Cruise Missile

What accounts for the brazenness of the Bush administration? For example, Paul Wolfowitz, the deputy secretary of defense, was talking about Syria, saying it was "behaving badly," like the head-master wagging his finger at the bad student.[7] How is this attitude seen outside the United States?

I think in two ways. On the one hand, it's seen as a kind of uncouth stupidity. On the other hand, it's seen as just the insulting language of power. You speak like that because you can.

In an interview you did in The Socialist Worker, *you said, "The greatest threat to the world today is not Saddam Hussein, it's George Bush (joined at the hip to his new foreign secretary, Tony Blair)."[8] Talk about Tony Blair. Why has he attached himself to American power with such fervor and vigor?*

That's a much more intriguing question than why the Bush regime is so brazen. The combination of stupidity, brutality, and power is an answer to the first question. But why is Blair behaving the way he is? I've been thinking about it, and my understanding is that what has happened is that the American empire has metamorphosed from the British empire. The British empire has morphed into the American empire. Tony Blair wants to be part of empire because that's where he thinks he belongs. That's

141

where his past, his country's past, has been, and it's a way of staying in the imperial game.

I was reading an article in *The New York Times* the other day that was appropriately called something like "Feeding Frenzy in Iraq."[9] It said that countries "representing their corporate interests" are bidding for subcontracts from Bechtel and Halliburton. Among the countries that are petitioning Bechtel and Halliburton, Bush administration officials said that Britain has the best case, because it "shed blood in Iraq." I wondered what they meant by that, because the little British blood that was shed was basically shed by Americans. And since they hadn't specified whose blood was shed, I presume they mean that the British shed Iraqi blood in Iraq. So their status as co-murderers means that they ought to be given privileged access to these subcontracts.

The article went on to say that Lady Symons, who is the deputy leader of the House of Lords, was traveling in the United States with four British captains of industry. They were making the case that they should be given preference not only because they were co-murderers but because Britain's had a long and continuous relationship with Iraq since imperial days, right up to the time of the sanctions, which means that they were trading with Iraq, were doing business in Iraq, through Saddam Hussein's worst periods.

The idea that you're actually trying to petition for privilege because you were once the imperial master of Iraq is unthinkable for those of us who come from former colonies, because we think of imperialism as rape. So the way the logic seems to work is, first you rape, then you kill, and then you petition to rape the corpse. It's like necrophilia. On what grounds are these arguments even being made? And made without irony?

What factor does racism play in this construction of imperial power?

Racism plays the same part today as it did in colonial times. There isn't any difference. I mean, the only people who are going to argue for the good side to imperialism are white people, people who were once masters, or Uncle Toms. I don't think you're going to find that argument being made by people in India, or people in South Africa, people in former colonies. The only ones who want colonialism back in its new avatar of neoliberalism are the former white masters and their old cohorts—the "native elites"—their point men then and now.

The whole rhetoric of "We need to bring democracy to Iraq" is absurd when you think of the fact that the United States supported Saddam Hussein and made sure that he ruled with an iron fist for all those years. Then they used the sanctions to break the back of civil society. Then they made Iraq disarm. Then they attacked Iraq. And now they've taken over all its assets.

The people who supported the military attack on Iraq may concede today, "Well, those reasons that we gave perhaps are not valid. We can't find the plutonium and uranium and biological and chemical weapons. Let's say we concede those points. But, after all, Miss Roy, we've got rid of a terrible dictator. Aren't the Iraqi people better off now?"

If that were the case, then why are they busy supporting dictators now all over central Asia? Why are they supporting the Saudi regime?

We're told that "Saddam Hussein is a monster who must be stopped now. And only the United States can stop him." It's an effective technique, this use of the urgent morality of the present to obscure the diabolical sins of the past and the malevolent plans for the future. This "present urgency" can always be used to justify your past sins and your future sins. It's a non-argument.

The Checkbook and the Cruise Missile

Islam is being targeted and demonized in much of the media, and also among what I can only describe as mullahs and ayatollahs here in the United States, people like Franklin Graham, son of Billy Graham, who called Islam "a very evil and wicked religion." Jerry Falwell said Mohammed was a "terrorist." Jerry Vines, who is a very prominent preacher, described Mohammed as a "demon-obsessed pedophile." [10]

This seems to integrate with a lot of the rhetoric coming from the Hindu nationalists in India, about Islam. Vajpayee said recently, "Wherever Muslims are, they do not want to live peacefully." [11]

The mullahs of the Islamic world and the mullahs of the Hindu world and the mullahs of the Christian world are all on the same side. And we are against them all. I can tell you that, insult for insult, you will find the mullahs in Pakistan or in Afghanistan or in Iran saying the same things about Christianity. And you will find the mullahs in India, and the RSS people in the Hindu right wing, saying the same things about each other. I see Praveen Togadia of the VHP and Paul Wolfowitz and John Ashcroft and Osama bin Laden and George Bush as being on the same side. These are artificial differences that we waste our time on, trying to figure out who is insulting who. They are all on the same side. And we are against them all.

Arundhati Roy and David Barsamian

You've traveled to the United States on several occasions. You give talks, and you meet and talk with lots of people. Why do you think Americans have been so susceptible to the Bush propaganda, specifically about Iraq being such an imminent threat to the national security of the United States, and that Iraq was responsible for September 11, and that Iraq is connected to Al-Qaeda, when there is simply no empirical evidence to support any of those assumptions?

I think on one level, the fact is that the American media is just like a corporate boardroom bulletin. But on a deeper level, why are Americans such a frightened people? After all, many of us routinely live with terrorism. If Iraq or El Salvador or Cuba is going to destroy America, then what is the point of all these weapons, these four hundred billion dollars spent every year on weapons, if you are that vulnerable in the end? It doesn't add up.

It's four hundred billion dollars a year, not including the Iraq war, which is a supplemental expenditure.

So what is it that makes a country with all these bombs and missiles and weapons the most frightened country and the most frightened people on earth? Why is it that people in a country like India, which has nothing in comparison, are so much less scared? Why do we live easier lives, more relaxed lives?

The Checkbook and the Cruise Missile

People are so isolated, and so alone, and so suspicious, and so competitive with each other, and so sure that they are about to be conned by their neighbor, or by their mother, or by their sister, or their grandmother. What's the use of having fifty percent of the world's wealth, or whatever it is that you have, if you're going to live this pathetic, terrified life?

Michael Moore's documentary "Bowling for Columbine" explores this to some degree.

What is wonderful about "Bowling for Columbine" is that it's accessible to ordinary people. It broke through the skin of mainstream media.

The language of the left must become more accessible, must reach more people. We must acknowledge that if we don't reach people, it's our failure. Every success of Fox News is a failure for us. Every success of major corporate propaganda is our failure. It's not enough to moan about it. We have to do something about it. Reach ordinary people, break the stranglehold of mainstream propaganda. It's not enough to be intellectually pristine and self-righteous.

There is a growing independent media movement in the United States, and it's connected with movements and organizations, such as

Arundhati Roy and David Barsamian

*Sarai.net in New Delhi, and Independent Media Centers all over
the world. There are a lot of young people getting involved in the media who are frustrated with the corporate pablum that they receive,
and they're doing something about it. You're in touch with some of
these activists in India.*

The fact that hundreds of thousands of people in the
United States were out on the streets, marching against
the war, was partly because of that independent media.
Unfortunately, it's not enough to walk out on the street
on a weekend. One of the things that needs to be done is
for the alternative media to reach a stage where the corporate media becomes irrelevant. That has to be the goal.
Not that you attack it, but that you make it irrelevant, that
you contextualize it.

*How do you develop the ability to discern fact from fiction in ap-
proaching news from mainstream outlets?*

I think the only way to do it is to follow the money.
Who owns which newspaper? Who owns the television
network? What are their interests? Assume that corporate
media has an agenda. And so the least you can do is to
cross-check a particular story with other sources of information that are independent. If you can do that, you can
see the discrepancies. Compare, for example, the way the

The Checkbook and the Cruise Missile

U.S. media and the British media covers the same war, the same event. How does this differ from how Al-Jazeera covers it? It's not as if these other media don't have an agenda. But if you look at the two, at least your head is not being messed with completely.

In the United States, there are a number of very well funded right-wing think tanks. And these think tanks provide many of the voices that are heard and seen in the media. For example, one of the most prominent is the American Enterprise Institute. Someone there—the holder of the Freedom Chair, incidentally—Michael Ledeen, said this, reported on the National Review *online: "Every ten years or so, the United States needs to pick up some small, crappy little country and throw it against the wall, just to show the world we mean business."*[12]

What can one say to that?

How are voices like this given such prominence in the media, while voices like Noam Chomsky or Howard Zinn or Edward Said or Angela Davis and others are completely marginalized?

But that's the project, isn't it? That's the Project for the New American Century. Why are we asking these questions or feeling surprised? We know that. And the brazenness of it is perhaps not such a bad thing. I'm for the brazenness, because at least it clarifies what is going on. And you know, you have to believe that eventually all empires founder, and this one will.

What about women's role in the globalization project? What factor does gender play?

That's not an easy question to answer. What if you were to reverse it and say, "What factor does gender play, vis-à-vis men?" Women are as complex as men, and different women benefit differently and suffer differently. So when it comes down to, say, the privatization of water, obviously, in an Indian context, it affects women much more than men, because they are the ones who have to walk not one kilometer, but fifteen kilometers now to fetch water. And that could be millions of women's whole lives, just going to scratch water out of some little place. To get just one pot of water, you could have to walk miles.

But it's not a question that I can answer that easily, because there are so many aspects to what we mean by globalization. The first half or more of my life was spent fighting the cruelties of tradition, dreaming of escaping from this little village that I grew up in, hoping that I wouldn't have to marry one of those men and produce children for them. And then I came up against the vulgarity of what modernity offers, and I had to refuse that, too, and walk a high wire, if you like, between the two. One is constantly, constantly making political choices.

And I am one of the lucky ones. Others don't have that choice, or don't see it that way, because sometimes what you are running from is so cruel that you can only run. This is a particularly complex subject, so let's just say that the project of corporate globalization increases the distance between those who make decisions and those who have to suffer them. Let's say neoliberal capitalism is a flawed machine. Inevitably, it leads to this huge disparity between the rich and the poor. And within the poor, it pushes women to the bottom.

Beyond the immediate excitement of being with people from many, many countries, what value is there in gatherings like the World Social Forum? Earlier you suggested that maybe we need to move beyond the marches and the typical demonstrations.

There's a tremendous value in the World Social Forum, and it has been central to making us feel that there is another world. It's not just possible. It is there. But I think it's important that we don't sap all our energies in organizing this event. It's an act of celebration of solidarity, but it's for us. It's not a strike against them. If you want to send out one million e-mails and enjoy the World Social Forum, you can, but let's reserve our energies for the real fight.

And that real fight is waiting to happen now. We need to clearly demarcate the battle lines. We cannot take on empire in its entirety. We have to dismantle its working parts and take them on one by one. We can't use the undirected spray of machine gun fire. We need the cold precision of an assassin's bullet. I don't mean this literally. I am talking about nonviolent resistance. We need to pick our targets, and hit them, one by one. It's not possible to take on empire in some huge, epic sense. Because we simply don't have the kind of power or reach or equipment to do that. We need to have an agenda, and we need to direct it.

At a press conference in New York, the day before your Riverside Church speech, you said, "We have to harm them." [13] *In what way can we harm them? Do we stop buying their cars? Do we stop traveling on their planes?*

First of all, we have to understand that we cannot be pure. You can't say, "Arundhati, if you are against empire, then why are you flying to America?" Because we can't do it in any virginal, pristine way. All of us are muddy. All of

152

us are soiled by empire and included in it in some way. We can only do our best. But certainly I believe that, for instance, a great starting point would be to target a few companies that have been given these reconstruction contracts in Iraq, and shut them down, just to show ourselves that we can do it, if nothing else.

If Bechtel or Halliburton was trying to establish some business in India, you would think that Indians should boycott them.

Absolutely—but also target their offices around the world, their other privatization projects around the world, target the CEOs, the members of the board, the shareholders, the partners, and let them know we will not allow them to profit off the occupation of Iraq. We need to disrupt business as usual.

The U.S. civil rights movement was ignited in 1955 by a bus boycott in the city of Montgomery, Alabama.

That's the thing. We need to be very specific now about what we have to do. Because we know the score. Enough of being right. We need to win.

You felt that the massive demonstrations on February 15 made a very powerful moral statement.

I think so. I think there was a huge difference between the display of public morality on the streets of the world and the vacuous, cynical arguments in the UN Security Council. We know all that talk about morality by old imperialists was rubbish. The minute war was announced, these supposed opponents of the war rushed to say, "I hope you win it." But I also think that the demonstrations and the peace movement really stripped down empire, which was very important. It stripped off the mask. It made it very clear what was going on. And if you look at general public perception of what the U.S. government is about, it's very different today. Not enough people knew what the U.S. government was up to all these years. People who studied it knew. Foreign policy scholars knew. Ex-CIA people knew. But now it's street talk.

The National Security Strategy of the United States of America, *which formally lays out the doctrine of preemption, actually has the statement in it that the events of September 11 presented the United States with "vast, new opportunities."* [14]

It did. Which is why I keep saying Bush and bin Laden are comrades in arms. But contained within those "opportunities" are the seeds of destruction. The fact is that here is an empire that, unlike other empires, has weapons that could destroy the world several times over

154

and has people at the helm of power who will not hesitate to use them.

What was the position of the Indian government on the attack on Iraq?

It was pretty inexcusable. There was a very subdued response to it in India. Because you see, the right-wing Indian government is trying very hard to align itself with the Israel–U.S. axis.

What do you mean by that?

Ariel Sharon is coming to India to visit quite soon. And the rhetoric against Muslims in the United States locks in with the fascist rhetoric against Muslims in India. Meanwhile India and Pakistan are behaving like the *begums* of Sheik Bush, competing for his attention.

Explain what "begum" means.

A *begum* is part of the sheik's harem.

How much of the traditional Orientalism that Edward Said has written about plays a factor in shaping and forming public opinion about the East, or "them," or "those people over there"?

I think outright racism would be a more accurate explanation. We are all expendable, easily expendable. Orientalism is a more gentle art. Crude racism powers all this.

Arundhati Roy and David Barsamian

You spoke in New York at the Riverside Church on May 13, 2003. How did you prepare for that, knowing that that church was where Martin Luther King gave his April 4, 1967, speech opposing the Vietnam War.

It was important to me to come to the United States and speak in that church. Apart from what I said in the talk, which is available as a text, there was a lot unsaid which was very political. A black woman from India speaking about America to an American audience in an American church. It's always historically been the other way around. It's always been white people coming to black countries to tell us about ourselves. And if anybody from there comes here, it's only to tell you about us and what a bad time we're having. But here is something else happening. Here citizens of an empire want to know what other people think of what that empire is doing. Globalization of dissent begins like that. That process is very, very important.

You've used the phrase "the checkbook and the cruise missile." What do you mean by this?

Once you understand the process of corporate globalization, you have to see that what happened in Argentina, the devastation of Argentina by the IMF, is part of the same machine that is destroying Iraq. Both are efforts to break open and to control markets. And so Argentina is destroyed by the checkbook, and Iraq is destroyed by the cruise missile. If the checkbook won't work, the cruise missile will. Hell hath no fury like a market scorned.

W.B. Yeats lamented in one of his most famous poems that "the best lack all conviction, while the worst are full of passionate intensity." I think when it comes to you, it's the exact opposite. You have that passionate intensity, and the total conviction. Thank you very much.

You're welcome, David. I am always happy to be flattered [laughs].

GLOSSARY

Adivasi: Tribal, but literally original, inhabitants of India.

Babri Masjid: On December 6, 1992, violent mobs of Hindu fundamentalists converged on the town of Ayodhya and demolished the Babri Masjid, an old Muslim mosque. Initiated by BJP leader L.K. Advani, this was the culmination of a nationwide campaign to "arouse the pride" of Hindus. Plans for replacing it with a huge Hindu temple (Ram Mandir) are under way.

Bajrang Dal: Hindu nationalist organization tied to the Bharatiya Janata Party and linked, along with the Vishwa Hindu Parishad, to the destruction of the Babri Masjid in Ayodhya in 1992.

Bharatiya Janata Party (BJP): A Hindu nationalist party (literally, the Indian People's Party).

Bhilali: The language spoken by an indigenous people in Central India.

Dalit: Those who are oppressed or literally "ground down." The preferred term for those people who used to be called "untouchables" in India.

Dargah: Muslim tomb.

Ganga: Ganges River.

Hindutva: Philosophy seeking to strengthen "Hindu identity" and create a Hindu state, advocated by the BJP and other communalist parties.

Hydel: Hydroelectric power.

Kargil War: A war India fought against Pakistan in 1999 in Kashmir.

Madrassa: A traditional Muslim school.

Malayalam: The language spoken in Kerala.

Mandir: Temple.

Masjid: Mosque.

Naga sadhu: A Hindu holy man.

Narmada Bachao Andolan (NBA): Save the Narmada Movement.

Parsis: Persian-descended Zoroastrians.

Ram Mandir: See the glossary entry for Babri Masjid above.

Rashtriya Swayamsevak Sangh (RSS): Literally, the National Self-Help Group. A right-wing Hindu cultural guild with a clearly articulated anti-Muslim stand and a nationalistic notion of hindutva. The RSS is the ideological backbone of the BJP.

Sahib: The Hindi word for "master."

Sangh Parivar: An overarching collection of Hindutva political and cultural organizations that includes the BJP, RSS, VHP, and Bajrang Dal.

Shakha: An RSS branch (literally) or center. RSS shakhas are "educational" cells.

Shiv Sena: A rabid right-wing regional Hindu chauvinist party in the state of Maharashtra.

Swadeshi: Self-reliance. Part of the Independence movement's call for the boycott of foreign goods and the establishment of home rule.

Tehelka case: An exposé by the Tehelka web site, in which senior Indian politicians, defense officers, and government servants were secretly filmed accepting bribes from journalists posing as arms dealers.

Bal Thackeray: The leader of Shiv Sena.

Vishwa Hindu Parishad (VHP): A right-wing Hindu group, which forms part of the Sangh Parivar.

Zamindar: Landlord.

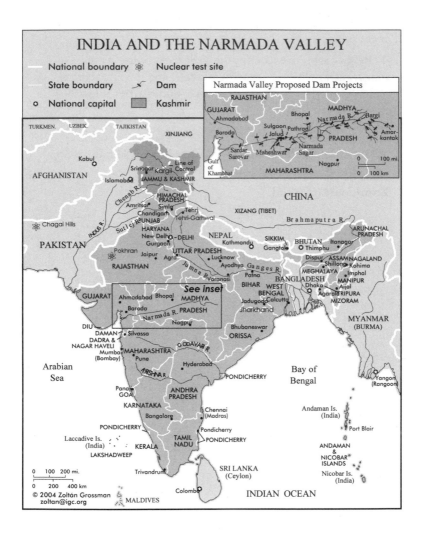

INDIA AND THE NARMADA VALLEY

— National boundary ❊ Nuclear test site

— State boundary ⚲ Dam

◎ National capital ▨ Kashmir

Narmada Valley Proposed Dam Projects

RAJASTHAN

GUJARAT
Ahmadabad

MADHYA
Bhopal
Narmada R.   Bargi

Baroda
Sulgaon Pathrad
Jalud   PRADESH
Amar-
kantak

Sardar
Sarovar   Maheshwar Narmada
Sagar

Gulf
of
Khambhat

Nagpur

MAHARASHTRA

0   100 mi.
0   100 km

TURKMEN. UZBEK. TAJIKISTAN

XINJIANG

Kabul
Srinagar Kargil   Line of
Control

AFGHANISTAN
Islamabad   JAMMU & KASHMIR

❊ Chagai Hills

PAKISTAN

HIMACHAL
PRADESH
Amritsar Simla
Chandigarh Tehri
PUNJAB   Tehri-Garhwal
HARYANA
New Delhi◎—DELHI
Gurgaon
❊ Pokhran   UTTAR PRADESH
Jaipur Agra
RAJASTHAN

CHINA

XIZANG (TIBET)

Brahmaputra R.

NEPAL
Kathmandu
SIKKIM
Gangtok

BHUTAN
◎ Thimphu

Itanagar
ARUNACHAL
PRADESH

Lucknow
Ayodhya Ganges R.
Varanasi   Patna
BIHAR

Dispur
Shillong
MEGHALAYA
NAGALAND
Kohima
Imphal
MANIPUR

Jumna R.

BANGLADESH
WEST   Dhaka
BENGAL   Agartala
TRIPURA
Aijal
MIZORAM

GUJARAT
Ahmadabad Bhopal
Baroda
See inset
MADHYA
PRADESH

Jadugoda Calcutta

Jharkhand

Narmada R. Nagpur

MYANMAR
(BURMA)

DIU
DAMAN
DADRA &
NAGAR HAVELI
MAHARASHTRA
Mumbai
(Bombay) Pune

Silvassa

GODAVARI R.

ORISSA

Bhubaneswar

Arabian
Sea

KRISHNA R.

Hyderabad

PONDICHERRY

Bay of
Bengal

Yangon
(Rangoon)

Panaji
GOA
ANDHRA
PRADESH

KARNATAKA
Bangalore

Chennai
(Madras)

Andaman Is.
(India)

Port Blair

PONDICHERRY

Laccadive Is.
(India)   KERALA
LAKSHADWEEP

TAMIL
NADU

Pondicherry
PONDICHERRY

ANDAMAN
&
NICOBAR
ISLANDS

0 100 200 mi.
0   200   400 km
© 2004 Zoltán Grossman
zoltan@igc.org   MALDIVES

Trivandrum

Colombo

SRI LANKA
(Ceylon)

INDIAN OCEAN

Nicobar Is.
(India)

NOTES

Foreword by Naomi Klein

1   Arundhati Roy, *Power Politics,* 2nd ed. (Cambridge, MA: South End Press, 2001), p. 126.

2   Arundhati Roy, *War Talk* (Cambridge, MA: South End Press, 2003), p. 112.

3   Roy, *Power Politics* 2nd ed., p. 127.

4   Arundhati Roy, "Do Turkeys Enjoy Thanksgiving?" *The Hindu,* January 18, 2004.

5   Roy, *War Talk*, p. 75.

6   Roy, this volume, p. 156.

7   Roy, *War Talk*, p. 83.

8   Roy, this volume, p. 30.

9   Arundhati Roy, *The Cost of Living* (New York: Modern Library, 1999), p. 12.

10 Roy, this volume, p. 14–15.

11 Roy, *War Talk*, p. 2.

12 Roy, *War Talk*, p. 75.

13 Roy, this volume, p. 154.

14 Roy, this volume, p. 152.

15 Roy, this volume, p. 153.

Arundhati Roy and David Barsamian

Chapter 1: Knowledge and Power

1   Nirmal Ghosh, "Indian Caste Killings Put Rule of Law to Test," *The Straits Times* (Singapore), August 10, 2001, p. 13.

2   Thirty large dams and many more small ones are proposed for hydro-energy production in the Narmada river valley. See Arundhati Roy, *Power Politics,* 2nd ed. (Cambridge: South End Press, 2001), p. 39.

3   The Communist Party came to power in Kerala in 1957.

4   "The Reproduction Function," *The Economist,* January 8, 1977, p. 72.

5   Arundhati Roy, *The God of Small Things* (New York: Random House, 1997; HarperPerennial, 1998).

6   The essays were published in 1993 and 1994 in the now-defunct *Sunday* magazine in India.

7   Abhay Mehta, *Power Play: A Study of the Enron Project* (Hyderabad, India: Orient Longman, 2000), p. 3.

8   See Roy, "Power Politics: The Reincarnation of Rumpelstiltskin," in *Power Politics,* 2nd ed, pp. 35–86, an updated version of an essay originally published in *Outlook* (India), November 27, 2000. See also Roy, *The Cost of Living.*

9   "India: Historians Flay Bid to Communalise History," *The Hindu* (India), November 7, 2001.

10 Roy, *The God of Small Things,* p. 14.

11 Roy, "The Greater Common Good," in *The Cost of Living.*

12 See The Friends of River Narmada, "The Sardar Sarovar Dam: A Brief Introduction," http://www.narmada.org/ sardarsarovar. html; "Sardar Sarovar Project—Denial of Rights!" http://www.narmada.org/sardar-sarovar/rr.feb 2002. html; and "Who Pays? Who Profits? A Short Guide to the Sardar Sarovar Project," http://www.narmada.org/ sardar-sarovar/faq/whopays.htm.

13 Bradford Morse et al., *Sardar Sarovar: The Report of the Independent Review* (Ottawa: Resource Futures International, 1992). See

also Robert Marquand, "Indian Dam Protests Evoke Gandhi," *Christian Science Monitor,* August 5, 1999, p. 1.

14 C.V.J. Sharma, ed., *Modern Temples of India: Selected Speeches of Jawaharlal Nehru at Irrigation and Power Projects* (Delhi: Central Board of Irrigation and Power, 1989), pp. 40–49.

15 R. Rangachari et al., "Large Dams: India's Experience: A WCD Case Study Prepared as an Input to the World Commission on Dams," Final Paper: November 2000, World Commission on Dams Country Review Paper, pp. 116–17 and 130–31. Online at http:// www.dams.org/studies/in/.

16 World Commission on Dams, *Dams and Development: A New Framework for Decision-Making: The Report of the World Commission on Dams* (London and Sterling, Virginia: Earthscan, 2000), Box 4.3, p. 104.

17 Roy, *Cost of Living,* p. 8.

18 In 2001, according to United Nations statistics, 72.1 percent of India's population was rural and India ranked 127th in the Human Development Index. United Nations Development Program (UNDP), *Human Development Indicators 2003,* Table 5 (Demographic Trends): Urban Population (as % of Total), http://www.undp.org/hdr2003/indicator/indic_41_1_1.html.

19 Roy, "The End of Imagination," in *The Cost of Living.*

20 Jason Burke, "Kashmir Feels Heat of Summer War," *The Observer* (London), June 6, 1999, p. 29.

21 Jonathan Braude, "Little Hitler Calls Shots," *South China Morning Post* (Hong Kong), November 13, 1995, p. 19; Peter Popham, "Why Indian Nationalists Would Love to Massacre St. Valentine's Day," *The Independent* (London), February 14, 2002, p. 16; and Peter Popham, "Valentine's Day 'Sullies Hindu Ways,'" *The Independent* (London), February 13, 2001, p. 14.

22 Roy, *Power Politics,* pp. 2–3.

23 Christopher Thomas, "Villages of the Dammed," *The Times* (London), May 11, 1991.

24 For more details, see Roy, "Democracy: Who Is She When She Is at Home," in *War Talk* (Cambridge: South End Press, 2003), pp. 17–44.

25 Roy, "The End of Imagination," in *The Cost of Living*.

Chapter 2: Terror and the Maddened King

1   Simon Holden, "Booker Winner Faces Morality Case in India," Press Association Limited, October 15, 1997.

2   Aradhana Seth, "DAM/AGE: A Film with Arundhati Roy," 50 minutes (Brooklyn, New York: First Run/Icarus Films, 2003). Originally produced for BBC 4, London, and aired April 2002.

3   Roy, "Come September," in *War Talk,* p. 46.

4   Michael Moore, "Bowling for Columbine" (New York: Metro-Goldwyn-Mayer, 2003).

5   Roy, *War Talk*, p. 52.

6   Roy, *War Talk*, p. 49.

7   Claudio Alvares, "The Bhopal Gas Disaster: Fresh Outrage," *Third World Resurgence* 143-44 (July–August 2002), pp. 12–13. Sabrina Jones, "Survivors Pressure Dow on Bhopal Aftermath," *Washington Post,* May 7, 2002, p. E6.

8   "'MP Govt. Misused Relief Funds,'" *The Statesmen* (India), February 22, 2001.

9   Roy, *Power Politics,* p. 138.

10 The White House, *The National Security Strategy of the United States of America* (Washington, D.C.: The White House, September 17, 2002), http://www.whitehouse. gov/nsc/nss.html. Madeleine Albright quoted in Noam Chomsky, "US Iraq Policy: Motives and Consequences," in *Iraq Under Siege: The Deadly Impact of Sanctions and War,* 2nd ed. (Cambridge: South End Press, 2002), p. 72.

11 Cited in Noam Chomsky, *Hegemony or Survival: America's Quest for Global Dominance* (New York: Metropolitan, 2003), p. 190.

12 Churchill quoted in Editorial, "Scurrying Toward Bethlehem," *New Left Review* 10, 2nd series (July/August 2001), p. 9, n. 5.

13 Roy, *Power Politics,* 2nd ed., p. 145.

Chapter 3: Privatization and Polarization

1 Noam Chomsky, *For Reasons of State,* updated ed., Introduction by Arundhati Roy (New York: New Press, 2003).

2 Dan Morrison, "India's 'Patriot Act' Comes Under Scrutiny," *Christian Science Monitor,* October 30, 2003, p. 7; Akshaya Mukul, "12-Year-Old Boy Arrested Under POTA," *The Economic Times of India,* February 21, 2003; Teesta Setalvad, "Do We Need Another TADA?" *The Times of India,* July 23, 2000.

3 Nirmal Ghosh, "New Delhi Mall Shootout: Police Credibility On Line," *The Straits Times* (Singapore), November 9, 2002; Agence France-Presse, "Pakistan Says Indian Mall Clash Fake, Refuses to Collect Bodies," November 11, 2002.

4 On October 29, 2003, Geelani was freed, after nearly two years in jail, when a New Delhi appeals court overturned his conviction. Edward Luce, "Indian Court Quashes Academic's Terror Conviction," *Financial Times* (London), October 30, 2003, p. 13; Morrison, "India's 'Patriot Act' Comes Under Scrutiny," p. 7; Amnesty International, "India: Open Letter to Law Minister about the Trial of Abdul Rehman Geelani and Three Others," July 8, 2002 (AI Index: ASA 20/011/2002 (Public), News Service No: 116, http://web.amnesty.org/library/index/ENGASA200112002.

5 Hina Kausar Alam and P. Balu, "J&K [Jammu and Kashmir] Fudges DNA Samples to Cover Up Killings," *The Times of India,* March 7, 2002.

6 Amy Waldman, "A Web Site in India that Revealed Graft Becomes a Target," *New York Times,* February 13, 2003, p. A5; Celia W. Dugger, "Bribery Scandal Engrosses TV Viewers in India," *New York Times,* March 24, 2001, p. A3.

7   Luke Harding, "Act of Desecration which Changed the Face of Indian Politics," *The Guardian* (London), March 1, 2002, p. 19; John F. Burns, "A Decade After Massacre, Some Sikhs Find Justice," *New York Times,* September 16, 1996, p. A4.

8   Roy, *War Talk,* pp. 17–44.

9   Agence France-Presse, "India, Enron Deny Payoff Charges Over Axed Project," August 7, 1995.

10 Roy, *Power Politics,* 2nd ed., p. 40.

11 Roy, *The Cost of Living,* pp. 50–51; Usha Ramanathan, "Along the Narmada...," Report of Public Hearings (*Jan Sunvayi*) from the Narmada Valley, July 13–15, 2002, www.narmada.org/ sardar-sarovar/jan.sunvayi.report.pdf; Christopher Kremmer, "The Flood of Outrage," *Sydney Morning Herald,* September 4, 1999, p. 6.

12 World Commission on Dams, *Dams and Development;* Stewart Fleming, "Damning of the World's Dam-Builders," *Evening Standard* (London), November 16, 2000, p. 45; Phil Williams and Patrick McCully, "Lies, Dam Lies," *The Guardian* (London), November 22, 2000, p. 8; Phil Williams, "Poor Are Sold Down the River," *Manchester Guardian Weekly,* December 13, 2000, p. 26.

13 Sanjay Kak, "Words on Water," 85 minutes (New Delhi, 2002).

14 George Eliot (Mary Ann Evans), *Felix Holt, the Radical* [1866] (New York: Oxford UP, 1980), p. 58.

15 "Speed Up Linking of Major Rivers: SC [Supreme Court] Tells Gov[ernmen]t," *The Times of India,* November 1, 2002; Medha Patkar and L.S. Aravinda, "Interlinking Mirages," *The Hindu* (India), December 3, 2002; Manoj Mitta, "The River Sutra," *Indian Express,* March 1, 2003.

16 Atal Behari Vajpayee quoted in Celia W. Dugger, "India Reacts With Anger to a Speech by Pakistani," *New York Times,* February 7, 2002, p. A9.

17   Amy Waldman, "New Government in Kashmir Brings Hope for Peace," *New York Times,* November 3, 2002, p. 1: 4.

18   "Nobel laureate Amartya Sen may think that health and education are the reasons why India has lagged behind in development in the past 50 years, but I think it is because of defence," said L.K. Advani. See "Quote of the Week, Other Voices," *India Today,* June 17, 2002, p. 13.

19   "VHP Calls Advani a Pseudo-Secularist," *The Hindu,* November 20, 2002.

20   *India Today,* November 18, 2002, http://www.india today.com/itoday/20021118/index.shtml.

21   Chomsky, *Hegemony or Survival,* p. 225–32.

22   Roy, *Power Politics,* 2nd ed., p. 30.

23   Frederick Douglass, "The Significance of Emancipation in the West Indies," in *The Frederick Douglass Papers, Series One: Speeches, Debates, and Interviews, Volume 3: 1855–63,* ed. John W. Blassingame (New Haven: Yale University Press, 1985), p. 204.

24   Muhammed Iqbal, *Bang-e-Dara* (1924), in *Kulliyat-e-Iqbal* (India: Aligarh Book Depot, 1975), p. 278. Translation by David Barsamian.

25   Prayas (Initiatives in Health, Energy, Learning and Parenthood), Pune, India, http://www.prayaspune.org/. See Rasika Dhavse, "Determined Efforts, Definite Direction," November 2002, Indiatogether.org, http://www.india together.org/stories/2002/rd1102.htm.

26   Martin Luther King, Jr., "Beyond Vietnam" (April 4, 1967). In Martin Luther King, Jr., Martin Luther King Papers Project at Stanford University, Stanford, California, http://www. stanford.edu/group/King/publications/speeches/Beyond_ Vietnam.pdf.

27   Martin Luther King, Jr., "Letter from Birmingham Jail" (April 16, 1963). In Martin Luther King, Jr., Martin Luther King Papers Project at Stanford University, Stanford, California,

http:// www.stanford.edu/group/King/popular_requests/
frequentdocs/birmingham.pdf.

28　"US Treasury Sec[retar]y Rubs it In: Reform, Reform and
Reform," *Indian Express,* November 22, 2002.

29　Lee Walczak and Richard S. Dunham, "Corporate Crime:
Why It's Not Sticking to Republicans," *Business Week* 3802
(October 7, 2002), p. 57.

30　Howard Zinn, *Terrorism and War,* ed. Anthony Arnove (New
York: Seven Stories Press, 2002), p. 55.

31　Ashutosh Varshney, "Doomed from Within," *Newseek,* March
18, 2002, p. 29; Maria Misra, "Religious Bigotry Is Poisoning
Indian Democracy," *Financial Times* (London), March 4, 2003,
p. 19.

32　Ben H. Bagdikian, *The Media Monopoly,* 6th ed. (Boston:
Beacon Press, 2000).

33　Bhaskar Roy, "Censor Board Bombards Peace Film," *The
Times of India,* June 23, 2002.

34　Noam Chomsky, *9–11,* ed. Greg Ruggiero (New York: Seven
Stories, 2001).

35　Thomas Babington Macaulay, "Minute of 2 February 1835 on
Indian Education," *Prose and Poetry,* ed. G. M. Young
(Cambridge: Harvard University Press, 1952), pp. 721–29.

36　*The New Yorker,* June 23 and 30, 1997.

37　Roy, *The Cost of Living,* p. 3.

38　Rashme Sehgal, "Female Foeticide Laves Haryanvi Grooms
Abegging," *The Times of India,* November 11, 2002.

39　Nargis is quoted in Salman Rushdie, "India's Courts Flounder
as Dam Pressure Builds," *Guardian* (London), August 11,
2001, p. 14.

Chapter 4: Globalization of Dissent

1　"Stray Incidents Take Gujarat Toll to 544," *The Times of India,*
March 5, 2002.

The Checkbook and the Cruise Missile

2   "Chinese Steel Firm Buys 50,000 Tonnes of World Trade Center Scrap," Agence France-Presse, January 23, 2002; "WTC Scrap at Gujarat Port Awaits Toxicity Test," *Indian Express,* April 17, 2002; L.H. Naqvi, "Workers Exposed to Toxic Ship Scrap," *The Tribune* (Chandigarh, India), June 2, 2003, http://www.tribuneindia.com/2003/20030602/biz. htm#1; Rinku Pegu, "WTC Wreckage for India: Exporting Toxins," February 1, 2002, Tehelka.com (India), http://www. tehelka.com/channels/currentaffairs/2002/feb/1/printabl/ ca20102wtcpr.htm.

3   See, for example, Niall Ferguson, "Welcome the New Imperialism," *Guardian* (London), October 31, 2001, p. 20, and Niall Ferguson, *Empire: The Rise and Demise of the British World Order and the Lesson for Global Power* (New York: Basic Books, 2003).

4   Thomas L. Friedman, "Bored With Baghdad — Already," *New York Times,* May 18, 2003, p. 4: 13.

5   Roy, *War Talk,* p. 111.

6   Andrew H. Card quoted in Elisabeth Bumiller, "Bush Aides Set Strategy to Sell Policy on Iraq," *New York Times,* September 7, 2002, p. A1. See Roy, *War Talk,* p. 66.

7   Paul Wolfowitz quoted in Walter Pincus, "Syria Warned Again Not to 'Meddle' in Iraq," *Washington Post,* April 11, 2003, p. A37.

8   Arundhati Roy, interview by Anthony Arnove, "'The Outline of the Beast,'" *Socialist Worker* 449 (April 13, 2003), pp. 6–7, http://www.socialistworker.org/2003-1/449/449_06_Arun dhatiRoy.shtml.

9   Elizabeth Becker, "Feeding Frenzy Under Way, as Companies from All Over Seek a Piece of the Action," *New York Times,* May 21, 2003, p. A18.

10 Nicholas Kristof, "Bigotry in Islam—And Here," *New York Times,* July 9, 2002, p. A21; Jerry Falwell, interviewed by Bob Simon, *60 Minutes II,* October 6, 2002.

11 Sanjeev Miglani, "Opposition Keeps Up Heat on Government Over Riots," Reuters, April 16, 2002.

12 Michael Ledeen quoted in Jonah Goldberg, "Baghdad Delenda Est, Part Two: Get On With It," *National Review* online, April 23, 2002, http://www.nationalreview.com/ goldberg/goldberg042302.asp.

13 Arundhati Roy, Press Conference sponsored by the Center for Economic and Social Rights, New York, New York, May 12, 2003. See also Roy, "Instant-Mix Imperial Democracy (Buy One, Get One Free)," New York, New York, May 13, 2003, http://www.cesr.org/Roy/ royspeech.htm, forthcoming in Arundhati Roy, *An Ordinary Person's Guide to Empire* (Cambridge: South End Press, 2004).

14 The White House, *The National Security Strategy of the United States of America,* Section VIII, "Develop Agendas for Cooperative Action with the Other Main Centers of Global Power," http://www.whitehouse.gov/nsc/nss.html.

INDEX

Arundhati Roy and David Barsamian

Union Carbide, 33, 49–50
  mentioned, 17, 29, 34, 50, 89,
    108–109, 112, 128
  court cases, 9, 41–43, 56–57, 80–82, 99

D

Dalits, 16, 24, 35, 61, 86, 127
dams
  Bargi Dam, 23
  Bhakra Dam, 76
  displacement due to, 2, 23–26,
    43–44, 54
  electricity, 91, 108–109
  irrigation, 17, 20–22, 24, 43
  Maheshwar, 34–35, 44, 83–84, 102
  Narmada valley, 13–17, 20–25, 33,
    56–57, 75–76
  privatization of water and, 20–22,
    76, 150
  Sardar Sarovar, 20–22, 24–25,
    34–36, 74, 83, 96
  World Commission on Dams, 25, 75
  See also agriculture; displacement
debt, 18, 76–77, 133
Delhi, 31–32, 79, 111, 132
  See also New Delhi
democracy
  decentralization of, 27, 73–74
  dissent in, 61–62, 79–81, 96, 103
  electoral, 2, 64, 78–79, 100, 114,
    131–132
  mockery of, 61–63, 79–81, 132,
    144
Devi, Phoolan, 10
displacement, 2, 23–26, 43–44, 74
  See also dams; resettlement policies
Douglass, Frederick, 98

E

economic sanctions, 93, 143–144
education, 2, 4, 7–8, 13, 122–123
electricity, 34, 91, 107–109
  See also dams
Eliot, T.S., 78

Empire (Ferguson), 137
Enron (corporation), 12, 27–29, 68,
  71–72, 108–109, 111–112

F

Falwell, Jerry, 145
farmers, 13, 18, 43, 76–77
Farukh, Abdullah, 85
fascism
  corporations and, 27, 71, 76–78
  Hindu, 51, 71, 88, 129–130, 134,
    155
Ferguson, Niall, 137–138
Ferozeshah Kotla, 32–33
fertility, 4, 125
feticide, 125
For Reasons of State (Chomsky), 59
Friedman, Thomas, 138

G

Gandhi, Indira, 63–64, 79
Gandhi, Mahatma, 110, 135
Gates, Bill, 108
Geelani, Syed Abdul Rehman, 62, 64
globalization
  communalism and, 29–30, 36, 77, 99
  corporate, 40, 77, 133–135, 151,
    156–157
  decentralization and, 27, 73–74
  privatization and, 29, 150
  psychology of, 55–56, 89–91
government
  censorship policies, 115–116
  compensation policies, 43–44, 50
  displacement policies, 2, 23–26,
    43–44
  infrastructure and, 12–13, 16,
    27–29, 34, 76, 78, 103, 107–109
  judiciary, 9, 79–81, 121
  language of, 12–13, 16–17,
    120–121
  resettlement policies, 25, 43, 74
  terrorism policies (U.S.), 51–54, 61,
    116–118, 138

174

Arundhati Roy and David Barsamian

Modi, Narendra, 63, 79, 105,
130–134
Mohammed, 145
Moore, Michael, 46, 147
Morse Report, 22
movies/films
  Bandit Queen, 10
  Bollywood racism in, 126–128
  Bowling for Columbine, 46, 119, 147
  DAM/AGE, 42, 56, 75–76, 121
  documentaries, 33, 76, 94,
    115–116, 147
  filmmakers, 42, 46, 76, 115–116,
    128
  rape protrayals in, 4, 10
  Roy's work on, 33, 42–43, 56,
    75–76, 116, 121
  Words on Water, 76
Musharraf, General Pervez, 53
Muslims, 49–51, 62–63, 94, 100,
  129–134, 145, 155

N

Naga sadhu, 17
Naipaul, V.S., 122
Nambodiripad, E.M.S., 2
Narmada Valley Development
  Project, 13–17, 20–25, 33, 35, 44,
  56–57, 75–76
  See also dams; displacement
nationalism, 28–30, 36, 39, 78, 88, 99,
  133, 135
NBA (Narmada Bachao Andolan),
  15–17, 33, 75, 83–84, 96
Nehru, Jawaharlal, 23
neoliberalism, 82–83, 91, 110–111,
  143, 151
  See also colonialism
New Delhi, 12, 30–31, 53, 56, 59, 62,
  75, 148
  See also Delhi
NGOs (non-governmental
  organizations), 82, 109
9–11 (Chomsky), 116

nuclear weapons, 28–30, 36–37, 52,
  55, 85, 101–102, 133

O

obscenity case, 9, 41–42
O'Neill, Paul, 111

P

Pakistan, 28, 39, 51–53, 62, 84–85, 99
Palestine, 47, 51, 53–54, 112
Partition (India/Pakistan), 39, 100,
  135
Patwardhan, Anand, 116
pesticides, 17–19, 76
political parties
  Bajrang Dal, 36, 88, 130
  BJP, 15, 21, 36, 86, 93, 100–101
  Communist, 1–3, 60
  Congress Party, 63, 79, 100, 132
  RSS, 1, 36, 76, 86, 100, 145
  VHP, 15, 35–36, 88, 130, 145
pollution, 3, 17–19, 76
PoTA (Prevention of Terrorism Act),
  61
power
  Douglass on, 98
  NGOs and, 82
  powerlessness and, 14, 26, 44–46
  truth known by, 12–15, 67–68, 115,
    118
press, the
  bias of, 67, 80, 94, 97, 113,
    115–116, 119, 148–149
  "free press," 48–49, 59–60, 71,
    115–117, 119, 139, 146–147
  inaccuracy of, 87
  independent media movement,
    147–148
  languages and, 132–134
  See also media
privatization
  corruption and, 72
  of electricity, 34, 91, 107–108
  globalization and, 29, 150

176

Arundhati Roy and David Barsamian

Seth, Aradhana, 42, 76
Shamir, Yitzhak, 53
Sharon, Ariel, 51, 155
Shiva, Vandana, 55
Sikhs, 62–63, 79, 132
SIN (Sweethearts International
Network), 67
"SLAPP" lawsuits, 80–82
South End Press, 65, 124
"speaking truth to power," 67–68, 118
specialization, 10–11, 18–19, 21, 27,
120–121, 135
suicides, 18, 76–77
Symons, Lady, 142
Syria, 139, 141
Syrian Christians, 2, 4

T

Tanzania, 19
Tehelka scandal, 63
television, 94, 97, 115, 126–127, 149
See also press
terrorism
economic, 89–93, 143–144
loss of freedoms and, 61–63
as privatization of war, 92
privileged, 52
UN resolution, 53
U.S. image and, 93, 114, 116–117
U.S. policies on, 51–54, 60–61, 83,
116–118, 138, 154
Thackeray, Bal, 29
Thakker, Himanshu, 124
Togadia, Praveen, 145
tribal people, 113

U

Union Carbide (corporation), 33,
49–50
unions, 3
United Nations, 53
United States
corporate crime wave in, 72,
111–112

culture, 17, 19, 46–53, 72, 94–95,
138, 146–147
elections, 114, 131
imperial power of, 50–51, 112, 135,
137–143
public awareness levels, 47–49,
115–117, 119
state terrorism of, 51–54, 60–61,
116–118, 138–140, 154
terrorist image of, 93, 114, 116–117
USA PATRIOT Act, 61
Uttar Pradesh, 2, 29, 129

V

Vajpayee, A.B., 53, 77, 88, 145
Venezuela, 140
VHP (Vishwa Hindu Parishad) party,
15, 35–36, 88, 130, 145
Vietnam, 59, 71, 156
Vines, Jerry, 145

W

water, 17, 20–22, 76, 150
See also dams
Wolfensohn, James, 75
Wolfowitz, Paul, 141, 145
women
resistance movements and, 44,
125–126, 150
treatment of, in India, 4, 10, 44, 84,
125, 130–131, 151
World Bank, 14–18, 22, 74–75, 92
World Commission on Dams, 25, 75
World Social Forum (Brazil), 139,
151–152
WTO (World Trade Organization),
11–12, 14, 18, 74, 76–77, 92, 94, 133

Y

Yeats, W.B., 157

Z

Zinn, Howard, 112, 149

178

ABOUT ARUNDHATI ROY

Arundhati Roy is the author of the novel *The God of Small Things*, for which she was awarded the Booker Prize in 1997, and three essay collections: *War Talk, Power Politics,* and *The Cost of Living.* Roy received the 2002 Lannan Award for Cultural Freedom. Roy was trained as an architect. She lives in New Delhi, India.

Photo © Paroma Basu

ABOUT DAVID BARSAMIAN

Photo © Sima Avakian

David Barsamian is the producer of the award-winning syndicated radio program Alternative Radio. A regular contributor to *The Progressive* and *Z Magazine,* Barsamian's most recent interview books include *Culture and Resistance: Conversations with Edward W. Said, Propaganda and the Public Mind: Conversations with Noam Chomsky* and *Eqbal Ahmad: Confronting Empire.* He lives in Boulder, Colorado.

ABOUT SOUTH END PRESS

South End Press is a nonprofit, collectively run book publisher with more than 200 titles in print. Since our founding in 1977, we have tried to meet the needs of readers who are exploring, or are already committed to, the politics of radical social change. Our goal is to publish books that encourage critical thinking and constructive action on the key political, cultural, social, economic, and ecological issues shaping life in the United States and in the world. In this way, we hope to give expression to a wide diversity of democratic social movements and to provide an alternative to the products of corporate publishing.

Through the Institute for Social and Cultural Change, South End Press works with other political media projects—Alternative Radio; SpeakOut, a speakers' bureau; and Z Magazine—to expand access to information and critical analysis.

Write or e-mail southend@southendpress.org for a free catalog, or visit www.southendpress.org.